OLD HONG KONG
IN COLOUR

OTTO C.C. LAM

PETER CUNICH has been teaching history at the University of Hong Kong since 1993. Although his main area of research is early modern English history, he has also written extensively on the history of European missionary activity in south China and the history of higher education in Hong Kong. He is the author of *Old Hong Kong* (2014) and for several years was editor of the *Journal of the Royal Asiatic Society Hong Kong Branch*.

OTTO C.C. LAM pursued a career in the fashion industry after his graduation from fashion college, but he started collecting rare books and photographs of Hong Kong and China after beginning to work for the UK fashion market in 1993. His study of the numismatic history of Hong Kong and China eventually resulted in a PhD in history from the University of Hong Kong. Although his main field of research is the early banking history of Hong Kong and China, he has taken a keen interest in the early colonial history of Hong Kong and missionary activity in China. Otto is a Museum Expert Adviser of Hong Kong, a member of the Hong Kong Sheng Kung Hui Archives & History Advisory Committee and a member of the Royal Numismatic Society. His latest publications include *Hong Kong in the Early Banking of China* (2016) and *Beyond Black & White – Colour Snapsots of Hong Kong in the 50s & 60s* (2018).

OLD HONG KONG IN COLOUR

Otto C.C. Lam

Introduction
Peter Cunich

Photograph repair
Chris K.K. Ma, Otto C.C. Lam, Eric Fok

Source of images
Otto C.C. Lam's Collection

Editor Lai Yiu Keung
Design Eric Fok
Print Production Lau Hon Kui

Published by Chung Hwa Book Co. (H.K.) Ltd.
Flat B, 1/F, North Point Industrial Building, 499 King's Road, North Point, H.K.
Tel : (852) 2137 2338 Fax : (852) 2713 8202
Email : info@chunghwabook.com.hk
Website : www.chunghwabook.com.hk

Distributed by SUP Publishing Logistics (H.K.) Ltd
3/F, C & C Buliding, 36 Ting Lai Road, Tai Po, N.T., Hong Kong
Tel : (852) 2150 2100 Fax : (852) 2407 3062
E-mail : info@suplogistics.com.hk

Printed by C & C Joint Printing Co., (H.K.) Ltd.
14/F, C & C Building, 36 Ting Lai Road, Tai Po, N. T., Hong Kong

Edition First Published in November 2018
©Chung Hwa Book Co. (H.K.) Ltd.

Format 304mm x 280mm

ISBN 978-988-8571-47-5

Contents

Introduction

Hong Kong – City of Colour
by Peter Cunich

We have become accustomed to the representation of Old Hong Kong through images in monochromatic tones of black, white and grey, but in its earliest phase of British occupation, the city was typically rendered in glorious full colour. These vibrant early images reflect the reality that Hong Kong was without doubt a colourful city – both figuratively and literally – from its founding days. While black-and-white engravings of the colony appearing in *The Illustrated London News* from the early 1850s became popular for a time, it was not until the widespread availability of black-and-white photographs of the colony from the early 1860s that colour renderings of Hong Kong became less common. Indeed, it is notable that some of the early *Illustrated London News* images of Hong Kong have survived only as coloured versions of their black-and-white originals, indicating that mid-nineteenth-century connoisseurs preferred representations that more faithfully reflected the realities of the world around them with respect to colour. This had certainly been the case up until the middle of the nineteenth century when paintings in colour had been the norm in Western art.

In South China, too, a flourishing business had arisen in Canton providing painted portraits and landscape scenes that allowed returning expatriates to remember their time in China nostalgically. Largely unknown Chinese artists were already at work in Hong Kong from the mid-1840s, accepting commissions from local merchants and government officials who wanted their houses, businesses, ships and the growing city of Victoria to be fixed on canvas so that these familiar scenes from the newest British settlement in East Asia could be taken back to Britain and remembered in retirement. Many of these paintings are pregnant with emotive force. The craggy northern face of Hong Kong Island rises threateningly out of the wine-dark waters of the harbour, the climate-scarred hills bare of any vegetation, but all along the praya the multicoloured structures of the infant colony are laid out with their small garden plots struggling for survival in the unaccustomed heat of South China. In one fine example of this genre, A.R. Johnston's green-shuttered record office is surrounded by luxuriant tropical palm trees with a shimmering light blue sky overhead. In other depictions of the harbour we see an assortment of sailing ships, the European vessels with their distinctive national flags picked out in bright colours while the Chinese junks are wallowing alongside with their billowing red sails. Even the native granite used in the construction of the harbourside office buildings and the palaces of the merchant princes in the Mid-Levels refused to be identified by its greyness, for in reality it often came in a variety of subtle shades of pink. This was no monochrome settlement on the fringes of civilisation; it was a thriving, exuberant, and many-coloured focal point of European activity in South China, just as Canton had been before it.

Until the early 1860s, photography had been a somewhat experimental and often less than precise attempt to capture the lineaments of the real world, despite its immediate appeal to travellers and diplomats with the means to practise the new science. While the first daguerreotypes of South China taken by Jules Itier in 1844 were both documentary and creative in purpose, they were not always technically sophisticated. They are perhaps best considered as curiosities rather than intrinsically desirable works of art. At least two professional photographers established short-lived commercial studios in Hong

Kong during the 1840s – George West in 1845-46 and Hugh Mackay in 1846-47, neither of whom have left any surviving work – but it was not until the late-1850s that photographic businesses in the colony became more popular and successful. The work of Leander Weed (1859-61), Felice Beato (1860-61), Milton Miller (1861-63), S.W. Halsey (1864-65), Jose Silveira (1865-67), William Floyd (1867-68) and John Thomson (1868-69) represent a true beginning of the photographic craze in South China, with the emergence of Lai Afong as the leading Chinese practitioner of the trade in 1870 marking the start of the heyday of black-and-white photography in Hong Kong. Although some photographers such as Beato experimented with hand-colouring their images to give them a more life-like appeal, a technique that would become popular in the production of postcards for tourists in the early twentieth century, the nineteenth-century world seems to have had the colour bleached out of it by the early 1860s. As elsewhere in the world, black-and-white photographs became the principal means by which people perceived the places that they had not visited themselves. As Gerard DeGroot has recently commented in *The Times* (4 August 2018), the period between 1850 and the 1960s has become a century in which our environment was 'imprinted on our consciousness in black and white, to the point where we imagine a monochromatic world ... etched in shades of grey'. Having absorbed the totalising greyness of this monochrome world, modern viewers find it quite unsettling to be confronted with coloured photographic images of this earlier black-and-white period, as Marina Amaral has attempted in *The Colour of Time* (2018). We are simply not accustomed to imagining the Victorian and early-twentieth-century periods in colour, and our accepted visual aesthetic is abruptly challenged by any attempt to transform these images to full colour, even though we of course know and understand that the world has always been as vivid and colourful as we perceive it today.

For this reason, the selection of photographs presented in this book may seem somewhat aesthetically jarring to readers who are familiar with the standard black-and-white photography of Old Hong Kong. This is a phenomenon that professional art photographers are familiar with, for since the development of colour photography in the 1930s, they studiously avoided colour for the next four decades. Although Cecil Beaton experimented with colour in his high-society photography of the late-1930s and Irving Penn used it to great effect during the Second World War, it was not until the 'explosion of colour' in the 1970s, brought about by rapid advances in technology, that colour photography earned a respected place in the realm of artistic expression. The reversible Kodachrome colour film that became available after the War was initially used largely for family and tourist photography, often noted for its amateurish naivety and spontaneous bad taste, so it is not surprising that professional photographers tended to avoid the use of colour in anything other than commercial photography. By the late 1960s, colour photography was still surprisingly absent from exhibition spaces. The Expo 67 thematic photographic exhibition in Montreal celebrated the modern 'age of the photograph' in which it was claimed that everyone was surrounded by photographs and nearly everyone made them, but somewhat surprisingly all these images were in black and white. Likewise, a late-1960s retrospective in Hong Kong covering the period 1954-1969 included just forty colour prints within a catalogue of more than 200 images, even though the rapid development of colour photography in the city was said to have made it one of the favourite hobbies of the general public. It was not until the 1970s that the sale of colour film surged, with worldwide black-and-white film purchases falling from 80 million in 1970 to less than 30 million by 1980. By the 1970s, then, the age of colour had arrived.

Colour photography in Hong Kong got off to a surprisingly slow start. Otto Lam has searched far and wide for the first colour photographic images of the city, but the earliest ones he has been able to date reliably were taken in the summer of 1948 by a visiting American journalist. It is known that amateur photographers such as Sir Lindsay Ride, vice-chancellor of the University of Hong Kong, were experimenting with colour photography by the early 1950s, so no doubt there were other local aficionados who joined in the craze during the 1950s, but the images they produced are difficult to unearth. Initially, photographers wishing to try colour photography would have had to purchase their film from overseas and then send it abroad for processing after it had been exposed. Colour processing eventually became more readily available in Hong Kong, but it was prohibitively expensive for the non-professional until the rapid technological advances of the 1970s. It is perhaps for this reason that around ninety per cent of the images in this book have come from private collections in North America, especially the United States, and virtually all of them are taken from transparencies. It was American tourists, so highly valued in post-war Hong Kong for their superior spending power, who could both afford to take holiday snaps in colour and had access to the processing facilities at home which enabled them to have the images developed with relative ease. One of the interesting cultural phenomena represented in this collection is the fact that most of the colour images of Hong Kong from the period 1948-1970 are 'foreign' in provenance, composition and previous ownership. They therefore represent an outsider's view of Hong Kong and give us a very good idea of what foreigners (especially those from North America) found interesting or novel when they disembarked from their cruise ships or, increasingly from the 1960s, their airliners, to experience the delights of 'the Riviera of the Orient'.

What, exactly, were these tourists expecting to find in Hong Kong? Many Americans would have had some general awareness of China, if not specifically Hong Kong, from the widespread coverage of the Pacific War in the American media. British visitors were probably better informed about the colony, with many of them visiting friends and relatives who had postings in the city, so they had greater access to 'local experience' when arranging their itineraries. Some tourists were probably returning to places they had previously visited either before or even during the war, but most were undoubtedly lured by the promise of being able to experience something of the 'mystical Orient' that was advertised so effectively by airlines, tour companies, and shipping lines. Although travellers had been coming to Hong Kong in large numbers since the early twentieth century, there was a quickening pace in tourism during the 1950s as more people gained access to international travel by sea or air. The local international passenger carriers, travel agents and tour operators banded together with hotel owners in 1957 to form the Hong Kong Tourist Association (HKTA), a body that sought to increase the number of visitors coming to Hong Kong from overseas, develop Hong Kong as a 'tourist destination', promote the improvement of visitor facilities in the city, publicise the tourist attractions in Hong Kong, and act as a lobbying group with the government to further the interests of the burgeoning tourism industry. They found that Hong Kong was not a difficult tourist destination to sell.

The HKTA was very successful in turning Hong Kong into a major international tourist destination in the 1960s, with passenger numbers arriving by sea and air increasing significantly between 1957 and 1967. Whereas there had been 667,000 passenger arrivals in 1947, dropping to only 576,000 in 1952 and 867,000 in 1957, the number of arrivals rose to 1.6 million by 1967. While it is difficult to determine with any accuracy how many of the earlier passenger arrivals were tourists, government statistics collected after 1957 indicate a rise in visitor arrivals from 103,000 in 1958 to 489,000 in 1967. Americans were always the largest single national group of visitors during this period, increasing from 35,000 in 1958 to 140,000 in 1967, while all British and Commonwealth visitors totalled only 33,000 in 1958 rising to 125,000 in 1967. Although the American share of the international tourist arrivals dropped slightly from 34% in 1958 to 29% in 1967, Americans were still the single largest group of foreigners to visit Hong Kong in the 1960s, while Japanese were the fastest growing group, increasing from only 6,000 in 1958 to more than 86,000 in 1967. By the late 1960s, local residents were beginning to notice that the city was awash with tourists; this was acknowledged as a good thing because of the economic benefits the industry was bringing to Hong Kong. Despite these increasingly successful promotional activities, however, Hong Kong was never turned into just another 'tourist city'. As Jan Morris has noted, the tourism 'industry' in Hong Kong continued to be 'all mixed up with everything else' in a multi-functioned and multicultural trading and industrial city, a situation that actually increased rather than diminished the interest of tourists in visiting the city.

Post-war Hong Kong was, in fact, a city that was experiencing a rapid transformation from the oriental entrepot of pre-war years, to the industrial powerhouse that it had become by the 1960s. When the British re-entered Hong Kong in September 1945 after nearly four years of Japanese occupation, the city had not quite been reduced to a pile of ruins, but much of the infrastructure had been destroyed by either enemy neglect or Allied bombing, and the population had plummeted from its pre-war peak of 1.6 million to little more than 600,000. By 1951, however, the infrastructure had been repaired and improved, and the population had risen to more than 2 million, with another million added by 1961. This rapid demographic growth was largely due to refugee arrivals from mainland China as people initially tried to escape the excesses of the civil war that raged from 1946 to 1949, and later sought to leave the country as successive political campaigns targeted various groups who were labelled as undesirable in the new People's Republic. A large wave of refugees therefore entered Hong Kong between 1949 and 1951, with another during the Great Leap Forward of 1958-61. The arrival of such large numbers of almost destitute and emotionally distraught Chinese refugees created a number of serious social problems for the colonial government to wrestle with, but it also provided a seemingly endless supply of cheap labour that could be used to fuel the industrial development of Hong Kong. The other factor that helped this process was the flight of industrial capitalists with their capital and expertise from Shanghai – they were to become the new industrial elite in Hong Kong from the early 1950s. The Hong Kong government ultimately decided to close its northern land border with China to prevent the colony from being swamped with Mainland immigrants, but by that time more than three million refugees had entered the colony. It might seem strange to think of such people as a tourist attraction, but it is evident from the colour photographs in this book that the plight of the Chinese refugees fascinated many overseas visitors.

Political changes in China also resulted in the expulsion of most foreign businessmen, missionaries and diplomats by 1951. Many of these people relocated to Hong Kong, at least initially, where they planned to await the eventual reopening of China. Some of them would still be waiting in the 1970s. As the Cold War intensified, Hong Kong became an important centre for China-watching, with a particularly large American presence. Regular visits by American naval vessels made the American military presence in the colony almost as prominent as the Royal Navy or the Gurkhas. The American Consulate on Garden Road

was said to be the largest American consular outpost in the world, with a significant CIA presence and the source of much propaganda work. Hong Kong in fact bristled with consulates of various nations, becoming known during the Cold War as 'the Berlin of the East'. The brooding presence of the largest Communist country in the world just a few miles to the north of Hong Kong's capitalist heart perhaps gave the city something of a frontier atmosphere, where no-one was ever sure what would happen next. Tourists certainly enjoyed the glamour of visiting the closed border area so that they could gaze across the barbed wire at Red China, but the experience seems to have been rather disappointing for most. All that could be seen beyond the Bamboo Curtain was farmland and an occasional farmer tending to the fields, but behind this bucolic idyll was the disturbing knowledge that People's Liberation Army troops had been stationed just across the border since 17 October 1949, prompting the British government to increase the Hong Kong garrison to 30,000 men. There were certainly moments of excitement, such as the siege at Sha Tau Kok in the early hours of 8 July 1967 when a Gurkha unit was called in to relieve the siege of a police outpost by 300 armed Chinese militia and protesters in which four policeman and one Chinese soldier were killed. Riots were also a not uncommon feature of post-war life in Hong Kong: the 1956 riots between pro-Beijing and pro-Taipei mobs in Kowloon left several dozen killed and hundreds hospitalised; the 1966 Star Ferry Riots in Central and Tsimshatsui resulted in one death and more than 1,000 arrests; the more serious six-month period of rioting that was instigated by Communist Party sympathisers in May 1967 left fifty killed and hundreds injured, with 5,000 arrests. Earlier in the 1950s, there had been a Cathay Pacific passenger aircraft shot down in 1954 and an Indian aircraft exploded shortly after take-off from Kai Tak airport in 1955, so throughout the 1950s and 1960s it was well understood that danger lay just below the surface of the relatively calm political situation in Hong Kong. It was partly because of this feeling of imminent danger that Ian Fleming commented in 1963 that Hong Kong was 'the most vivid and exciting city I have ever seen'.

Much of the tension in Hong Kong was not, however, political. It arose instead from the appalling conditions that Chinese refugees were forced to live in throughout most of the 1950s and 1960s. There was never enough housing for all the refugees so most of them literally took to the hills and constructed their own squatter shacks from discarded timber and kerosene tins as close to transport hubs as possible. The living conditions in these sprawling temporary settlements were rudimentary, with little provision for water, electricity or waste removal. The government initially did very little to regulate or provide services for these areas, but church groups and overseas aid agencies did what they could to supply minimal social and educational relief to the residents. As

the squatter settlements grew in size and spread to various locations across Kowloon and Hong Kong Island, they were recognised in some quarters as a howling indictment of the city's economic growth, but most simply turned a blind eye to the appalling conditions just beyond their doorsteps. Disease was rife, poverty omnipresent and violent disputes common, but the people who lived in these squatter settlements were proudly self-sufficient and hopeful of a brighter future if they just worked hard enough and made the most of the opportunities that Hong Kong offered. Such hopes were dashed for 58,000 people in Shek Kip Mei on Christmas Day 1953, when an all-consuming fire destroyed an entire hillside of squatter huts. This disaster prompted the government to step up a squatter resettlement programme, resulting in the construction of dozens of multi-storey residential blocks across the territory offering each family a small cubicle with communal facilities for washing, bathing and cooking. It was not much, but over the next twenty years the ambitious rehousing programme offered tens of thousands of families a more or less permanent home with a minimal level of comfort. Many people today associate the resilient 'Lion Rock outlook' of Hong Kongers from this period with the hard work and communal living that was such a prominent part of life in the city. By the mid-1960s, 30% of the population was living in government housing of one sort or another.

Any tourist who strayed far enough from the normal beaten track to see these housing estates would have been surprised at the very large number of children to be seen at all hours of the day and night. Indeed, wherever the tourist went in Hong Kong there were children to be seen, whether playing in the streets or on the waters of the harbour, or hawking various foodstuffs and trinkets. Many of the images in this book contain children and young people engaging in a range of activities – most of the subjects clearly come from disadvantaged backgrounds. By the late 1960s, half the population was under the age of twenty-one, with most of these youngsters bound for industrial jobs in the factories that were springing up everywhere at the time. Many children initially worked with their parents trying to scrape together a modest living before graduating to salaried employment in textile or plastic goods factories. Education was not compulsory, but it was keenly sought after by those who could afford it as a means to raise their children out of the poverty and distress that they had experienced during their time in Hong Kong. Very few tourists ever managed to penetrate into this darker side of life in Hong Kong. There is a complete absence in this book, for example, of photographs showing work in factories or the living conditions inside the government resettlement blocks. This is unfortunate, because these are the places where most people spent most of their lives. Again, the outsider's gaze is not the version of the past that the modern social scientist would desire in order to establish a full and balanced view of life in Hong Kong during the 1950s and 1960s, but there are enough photographs of the less privileged citizens in this collection to provide at least a glimpse of what life was like for most Hong Kongers at this time.

These photographs also reveal what international tourists were interested in seeing during the 1950s and 1960s. In fact, it is possible to recreate the itinerary of a typical overseas visitor from the moment of disembarkation at the wharves in Tsimshtsui or the airport at Kai Tak, until departure for the next leg of their holiday after a few days of sightseeing and shopping. Most tourists stayed in hotels around Tsimshatsui, which by this time had already become the centre of the tourism industry in Hong Kong. Whether wallowing in the internationally acclaimed luxury of the Peninsula Hotel, or enduring the less obvious attractions of smaller establishments scattered across the Kowloon peninsula, they all followed a similar path as they explored the city. Most would have hailed a rickshaw to or from the Star Ferry terminus, or the conveniently located ranks in Nathan Road and Canton Road. Crossing Victoria Harbour on one of the old ferries was like going back in time, with strictly separated first and second-class areas that reflected the wider social distinctions in the colony. The Northern Star, constructed in 1900, was still plying the waves until 1959, while the Golden Star (1928) and the Electric Star (1933) had been resurrected from the deep after the war and were kept in service until 1968. Newer 576-seat ferries were introduced from 1956, so that by the end of the 1960s a fleet of eleven modern vessels carried tens of thousands of workers and tourists each day. What was lost in historical ambiance was gained in modern comfort.

Once in Central, visitors took in the sights of the main business district with its wide streets and fine old buildings in a variety of styles of neo-classicism that had been constructed on the central reclamation in the early part of the century. Some may have been invited to lunch or dinner at the gentile Hong Kong Club, while others tasted the delights of the many Chinese restaurants that catered for visitors by the 1960s. The intrepid tourist might have headed off west along Queen's Road towards the old Chinese quarter, with its crowded tenements, teeming street life, and the Aladdin's-cave curio shops that sold all manner of Chinese antiquities, but the less daring chose the vertiginous excitement of the Peak Tram. This excursion would allow the visitor to experience the cooler climate of the Peak district, home to the wealthiest taipans and businessmen, with its panoramic views of the harbour to the north and the South China Sea to the south. Another favourite destination on the island for both locals and tourists was Tiger Balm Garden in Tai Hang. Tourists were conveyed to this extraordinary mixture of formal garden and garish Chinese mythical theme park by any number of tour operators, who also

offered trips to the south side of the island: Repulse Bay, for swimming and tea at the fashionable Repulse Bay Hotel, Stanley and its war cemetery, and the old fishing village of Aberdeen, where the harbour life and floating restaurants left an unforgettable impression on visitors.

Some visitors – perhaps those associated with foreign aid organisations – evidently took an interest in Hong Kong's social problems, for they valiantly sought out the teeming refugee masses in the squatter camps and resettlement areas. Few tourists had the time or inclination to visit the outlying islands or the villages of the New Territories, but those who did discovered places where time seemed to stand still, with elderly residents still practising traditional trades and crafts which would soon disappear forever. The ultimate in excitement would have been a visit to the closed border area to the distant north, and the possibility of spying real communists or soldiers of the PLA. Wherever they went, these determined visitors would carry their cameras, taking photographs of all the amazing scenes that unfolded before them, until they returned to their hotels, exhausted and footsore, but buzzing with excitement about what they had discovered in this most fascinating of cities.

What, then, is the value of these colour photographs? Perhaps the first characteristic that needs to be emphasised is the very different compositional aesthetic that seems to inform what are essentially casual shots of 'life in the raw'. The earlier black-and-white photographs of Old Hong Kong were much more purposefully composed than these amateur colour images. The pre-war photographs of buildings and other places of interest are usually devoid of any human activity, so it is clear that the photographers waited until they had the 'perfect shot' before releasing the shutter. The images that do include people are usually either formal portraits or else groups of people taken in physical settings that had significance for them. In either case, the images are posed rather than natural. The number of black-and-white images that could be classified as snap-shots of everyday life are few and far between. For this reason, the surviving black-and-white photographs of Old Hong Kong tend to be rather formal in their aesthetic. The post-war colour images are entirely different. They were usually taken in a hurry by tourists who were scrambling from one attraction to another and therefore had very little opportunity or desire to wait for a perfect shot. These images are therefore very much of the moment, and generally record everyday places and activities which appealed to the foreign photographer as unusual and interesting. While some are certainly posed, the composition is casual or mock-formal rather than the staid formality of the previous generation of black-and-white images. The purpose of the majority of these photographs was probably simply to preserve the fleeting memories of a visit to one of the world's most

exciting cities so that they could be shown to friends and relatives 'back home', or perhaps used entirely as personal mementos during times of nostalgic remembering. In this sense, they have a close affinity with the earlier China coast paintings of the nineteenth century.

This is not to say that the images captured by tourists in the 1950s and 1960s have only personal value. There are many photographs in this collection that record particular buildings or sites that were demolished long ago, so in this respect they constitute part of a larger body of evidence that can be used to chart the development of Hong Kong's urban landscape. A number of the images are also precisely dated, so the diligent urban historian is able to arrange photographs from different dates in a chronological sequence to assess how buildings in the city changed over time, all in full colour. While few of these photographs are truly unique – many other images of the same subjects exist – together they form a unique opportunity to trace developments over time through a visual record. Perhaps one unique element is to be found in the local people whose likenesses have been caught on film, especially the children who appear in the photographs. Many of these people would not have been able to afford photographs in the 1950s and 1960s, so it is possible that some may still be living today who will find unique and personally valuable images of themselves in these pages. Perhaps more historically significant is the series of photographs in Chapter 1 taken by an unidentified American visitor who carried his camera with him on a Kowloon-Canton Railway journey to Guangzhou in the summer of 1948. These colour images really are unique, showing the Guangdong countryside to the north of Hong Kong as it was just a year before the Communist victory in 1949. The traditional way of life captured in these images would change dramatically in the decades that followed, leaving little visual record of how life had once been.

In one sense, then, these colour images represent an important part of the visual historical record of Hong Kong's past. As the organisers of the 1967 Montreal photographic exhibition suggested, the camera is 'a most important witness to the past' and 'photography is the visual vernacular of our day'. While historians have often failed to realise the value of photographic evidence, amateur photographers have been collecting historical data with their cameras since the late nineteenth century, often in a very organised way. Many of the most important geographical and urban photographic collections held in British archives today spring from 'county photographic surveys' which were initiated by amateur photographers from the 1880s through to the 1930s in an effort to preserve some memory of landscapes and cityscapes that were rapidly changing as the Industrial Revolution and rapid urbanisation changed the face of Europe.

These collections are all composed of black-and-white images, as is Hong Kong's only photographic collection formed as a result of a similar effort by amateur photographers. The Royal Asiatic Society's late-1970s project to record the city's rapidly disappearing buildings west of Pottinger Street might have been expected to make use of colour photography, but it was evidently thought that black-and-white images were the only acceptable way of recording the past. The colour photographs in this volume were produced far more haphazardly than those in the RAS collection, but they are just as important in their own way as a witness to history. They mostly record the mundane and everyday things that tourists saw in Hong Kong during the 1950s and 1960s, so their focus is on the 'small players' in history, but herein lies their value. They record the real world of life in Hong Kong in all its unorganised and messy variety, not the imagined world of professional photographers trying to capture an image that told a preconceived story to a particular audience. The amateur photographers who recorded these images were unsuspecting witnesses to history, but it is only today that we are beginning to appreciate the value of these everyday images as Hong Kong struggles to remember a past that is receding from the collective memory all too rapidly.

In the pages ahead, almost every element of life in Hong Kong in the 1950s and 1960s is represented, together with a small selection of images of Guangzhou and Macau. Indeed, many of the images here would fit comfortably into one or more of the forty-nine categories that recorded the 'visual vernacular' of the modern world at the 1967 Montreal exhibition: children, young people, farming, fishing, family life, food, men at work, people, poverty, 'in the street', friendship and old age. The tourist 'camera as witness' has preserved for all time those fleeting moments of daily life that are often remembered with a halo of nostalgia but can never be reconstituted with full accuracy. This is not to say that these tourist photographs represent a complete record of Hong Kong at that time. Missing are images of industrial workspaces, the interiors of homes, and the sexual licence that was so prominent a feature of Hong Kong's international reputation after 'The World of Suzie Wong' was screened in 1961. But we have here the beginnings of a more comprehensive collection that needs to be assembled before the surviving colour transparencies of this period either disappear through neglect or deteriorate in quality with the inexorable action of time and climate.

The colour images in this book provide us with a final glimpse of Old Hong Kong, for the 1950s marked the beginning of the end for much of what had constituted the urban fabric of the city since the early twentieth century. Unlike the other historically important East Asian port cities, which fell into rapid decline after the Second World War, Hong Kong's thriving new industrial and commercial enterprises meant that it regained its former wealth and dynamism in the 1950s and 1960s. The profits generated in the post-war period allowed landowners and developers to build modern skyscrapers to replace the dignified but tattered older buildings in the city. In contrast, historical centres like Malacca, Penang and Macau became post-war sleepy hollows where large areas of the old urban fabric would be preserved through benign neglect, allowing their city governments in the next century to apply for World Heritage status for the carefully delineated 'heritage cores' of the old cities. Even in Canton, much of the early-twentieth-century city remained intact until the 1990s, including the former foreign concession of Shameen Island, which has today been completely restored to its former capitalist glory. In Hong Kong, the rapid demolition of buildings meant that the city very quickly lost its old core, leaving only a few of the older buildings scattered incongruously among the gleaming new towers.

Already in the early 1950s a number of historically significant buildings in Central had been demolished, but the 1960s saw an acceleration of this process. The last remnants of City Hall disappeared in 1949 to make way for the new Bank of China building in 1951, and Hong Kong Land erected the Edinburgh Building in 1950 on a site previously occupied by two venerable buildings from the late nineteenth century. The company was soon able to raise the capital necessary to replace its entire stable of stately classical edifices with a group of efficient but ugly modern doppelgangers: the Alexandra Building was demolished in 1952, the Royal Buildings in 1953, the King's and York Buildings both went in 1958, the Union Building in 1962, the Queen's Building in 1961, and the old Prince's Building in 1963. Only the Gloucester Hotel remained until the next decade, finally succumbing to the wrecker's ball in 1977. Elsewhere, the Hong Kong Hotel was demolished in 1952, Jardine House and the New Oriental Building were both lost in 1955, the Queen's Theatre in 1958, the Butterfield and Swire Building in 1960, the P&O Building in 1961, and the King's Theatre in 1962. The gloriously eccentric General Post Office remained until 1977 before making way for the MTR's Central Station, while the Hong Kong Club Building lasted a little longer, eventually being demolished amid much controversy in June 1981. Today, all that remains of the fine set of early-twentieth-century buildings in Central are the old Supreme Court building (now the Court of Final Appeal) and the French Mission Building. While the colour photographs in this book will not bring back the world that Hong Kong has lost over the last half-century, they at least provide a reminder to us of a city that many of us never knew.

The growing cross-generational thirst for images such as these is testament to the fact that Asia's World City has not yet forgotten its past despite the loss of virtually the entire physical presence of Old Hong Kong. Weekly newspaper stories about heritage issues, increasingly frequent calls on the public to assist in saving portions of Hong Kong's remaining tangible and intangible heritage, and belated but nevertheless welcome government programmes to document and protect the city's historic buildings and monuments mark a real shift in public engagement with the past. These colour photographs from the 1950s and 1960s will perhaps make Old Hong Kong a little more accessible to the twenty-first-century reader and encourage other collectors to save for the future those seemingly unremarkable colour snapshots from the post-war period.

Acknowledgements

The colour photographs of Hong Kong from 1948 to the 1960s in this book are from my private collection, and have been previously published in a Chinese version earlier this year. After the book was released, there was a strong demand for an English edition, so an enlarged English version has been prepared with support from the publisher and Dr. Peter Cunich, who kindly reviewed the entire text and wrote an introduction. I am indebted to Dr. Cunich for his help and advice in getting the English version into print.

I would like to record my thanks to Mr. Chris K.K. Ma, who offered invaluable assistance in repairing the photographs, mostly taken from the original slides which have various deficiencies. The quality of the photographs selected for the book owes a great deal to Chris's professional support. Special thanks are also due to my family and children for their love and patience while I indulged myself in this challenging task.

Last of all, for whatever blemishes and shortcomings that may still be found in the book, I alone remain responsible.

Otto C.C. Lam
21 October 2018

Chapter 1

The Appearance of Colour Photography in South China – Summer 1948

It took more than a century for colour photography to appear in China after the earliest photograph was taken in Macau by Jules Alphonse Eugene Itier, a French missionary, in 1844. Colour photography was limited to experimentation and laboratory tests until commercial colour film was developed by Agfa and Eastman Kodak in the 1930s. It seems that the adoption of colour film was not common before World War II. The cost of colour film and its processing were expensive compared with black-and-white film, which continued to be predominant among both professionals and amateurs in Hong Kong after the War and into the 1950s.

The commander of the Allied Forces in Hong Kong occasionally brought American soldiers and reporters with their Kodachrome colour film to East Asia. One resulting series of early colour photographs of Hong Kong and South China was taken by an American who worked for the BBC, and who traveled all the way from Japan and Korea via Hong Kong to Canton (Guangzhou 廣州). His journey through South China began with the Kowloon Canton Railway (KCR), travelling from the Tsimshatsui terminus in Kowloon through to Nangang (南崗). He took several photographs through the window of his KCR train at Tai Po Kau (大埔滘), showing farmland and paddy rice fields from Fanling (粉嶺) to Sheung Shui (上水).

The American photographer appears to have enjoyed his train journey along the China section of the KCR line. Photographs show that he passed through the station at Dashengcun (大盛村) where he took photographs of a horse farm with a view of the pagoda at Lianhuashan (蓮花山) in the background. It seems that he stopped off at a small station near Nangang, making a cross-country expedition by car towards Canton city. Shots were taken at parks and a town in Canton. Another image of the Zhongshan Memorial Hall (中山紀念堂) was taken from the car on his way to the airport before he finished his short visit to South China. These photographs of South China may be the only surviving photographic record taken in colour before Canton fell into the hands of the Communists in October 1949.

A group of aerial photographs demonstrates that the American photographer was on board a Douglas DC-3 aeroplane owned by the China National Aviation Corporation (CNAC) when flying from Canton to Hong Kong[1]. He took these photographs through the window on the right-side rear seat (probably the last or seventh window seat). They show the plane flying away from Canton along a winding river (the main Zhujiang (珠江) river near Lianhuashan) with a pagoda towering over the rice fields. The aircraft then turned towards Dongguan and flew over the Zhujiang delta. An aerial photograph taken over the Xiancun (仙村), Zhongtang (中堂) and Haixinzhou (海 心 洲) area shows the winding river shaped like a dragon, and then, approaching Hong Kong, he took a photograph over Stonecutter's Island (昂船洲)before coming in to land at Kai Tak airport in Kowloon.

The key part of the collection consists of several early colour images taken around the major tourist spots in Hong Kong during the hot summer of 1948: a Star Ferry crossing of Victoria Harbour to Central from the KCR rail terminus in Tsimshatsui, Chinese junks and sampans in the harbour, boats anchored near the King's Building off the Central praya, fisherman with fishing nets near the Connaught Road praya, the HSBC building, women talking loudly while eating sugar cane near the Royal Naval Dockyard, views of Victoria Harbour from the Peak, a panoramic view from inside the Peak Café, and a few photographs of Tiger Balm Garden including some colourful porcelain statuary just erected and a small pagoda carrying the national emblem of the Republic of China.

Having completed his tour, the American photographer flew to Manila at the conclusion of his visit to South China and Hong Kong[2]. He took with him the Kodachrome colour film which was eventually processed in the USA, where they were kept in a private collection for another seventy years before reappearing for the appreciation of a new generation of Hong Kong people.

1

China National Aviation Corporation (CNAC) was established by the National Chinese Government in 1929. Its ownership changed in 1933, with a 55% share kept by the National Government and the balance belonging to the US Aviation Corporation under the supervision of China Airways Federal Inc. CNAC mainly used US Douglas planes. Between 8 and 10 December 1941, seventeen days before Hong Kong fell into the hands of the Japanese occupation forces, American pilots of CNAC made a total of sixteen trips between Kai Tak Airport and Chungking in order to evacuate 275 persons, including Soong Ching-ling (the widow of Sun Yat-sen), and the Chinese Finance Minister H.H. Kung.

2

The CNAC flight path from Hong Kong to Manila was a new route developed after 1933. After the war, CNAC headquarters moved back to Shanghai Longhua airport until it ceased operations in November 1949.

1.1

A British War Department Austerity 2-8-0 steam locomotive No.22 for passenger train services was acquired by the Kowloon Canton Railway from London in 1947. This photograph was taken in 1955, but shows the same type of locomotive used by the KCR in the summer of 1948.

1.2

'From the train window approaching Tai Po
Kau, summer 1948.'

1.3
A farmer working his fields between Fanling and Sheung Shui station in the summer of 1948.

1.4

A whole family helping to plant rice near
Sheung Shui. The group slowly advanced
across the field as each row was planted.
Summer 1948.

1.5

The China section of KCR near Nangang in the Huangpu area. The train is passing a horse farm next to a wide river (Zhujiang) with a pagoda standing lonely in the distance (Lianhuashan Tower). Summer 1948.

1.6

Driving by car from Nangang to Canton, the photographer met with a farmer's cart-wagon commonly found in southern China at the time. Summer 1948.

1.7

'At the stops people flocked to the train with tempting trays of fruit, roast duck, and boiled duck eggs for sale. Many beggars cried for alms. As we pulled away from this stop an old man fell on the track and was killed.' Summer 1948.

1.8

'A truck filled with grain broke open slightly and these children scampered madly about picking up the kernels, Canton China. Summer 1948.'

1.9

These slick black oil-cloth suits (Heong Wan Sa, 香雲紗) were worn by many men and women in the area around Shunde and beyond. The man in white, probably a railway station employee, waves to the photographer, perhaps indicating that no pictures should be taken. Summer 1948.

1.10

A popular park in Canton, summer 1948.

1.11

'Looking back from my three wheeled bike, much like the one on right background, Canton , China, summer 1948.'

1.12

On the way to Canton airport, the car passed this beautiful building with a bright blue porcelain roof (Zhongshan Memorial Hall, 中山紀念堂). Summer 1948.

1.13

On the flight from Canton to Hong Kong, looking out of the rear window of a Douglas DC-3 plane, along a winding river with a pagoda towering over rice fields (the Lianhuashan pagoda). Summer 1948.

1.14

The plane turned towards Dongguan over winding rivers shaped like a dragon. In the centre is Xiancun（仙村）, with Zhongtang（中堂）on the left, Giaobu and Shijie（石碣）below, and Shilong（石龍）on the right. The dark line running across the photograph is the KCR railway line from Kowloon to Canton. Summer 1948.

1.15

Approaching Hong Kong – looking south to the mountainous Hong Kong Island across Stonecutter's Island. The Douglas DC-3 aircraft was coming in for a landing at Kai Tak airport in Kowloon. Summer 1948.

1.16

'The boys had just climbed into the bus thinking all the passengers had left the plane when an Indian woman came to the door and started down – the boys came to help her, Fall 1948.'

1.17

'City playground – one night I stayed at (Jordan) Hotel with Awnings – second floor this corner, Summer 1948'. A view from King George V Memorial Park in Kowloon towards Jordan Road with a path running through the park to Canton Road. The Jordan Hotel, located at the junction of Jordan Road and Ferry Street, survived from 1948 until the mid-1950s.

1.18

Leaving Kowloon on the Star Ferry, near
the KCR terminus. Summer 1948.

A Chinese family onboard a small fishing
boat. Summer 1948.

1.20

A high-sterned Chinese junk with heavy ribbed sails, taken from the Star Ferry, Summer 1948'

1.21

Map of the city of Victoria, Hong Kong, published by the Far East Printing Press and inserted inside *Hong Kong - A Guide Book on the Gem of the Orient*, 1953. The early colour photographs taken along Connaught Road show some of the buildings on this map as they were in the summer of 1948.

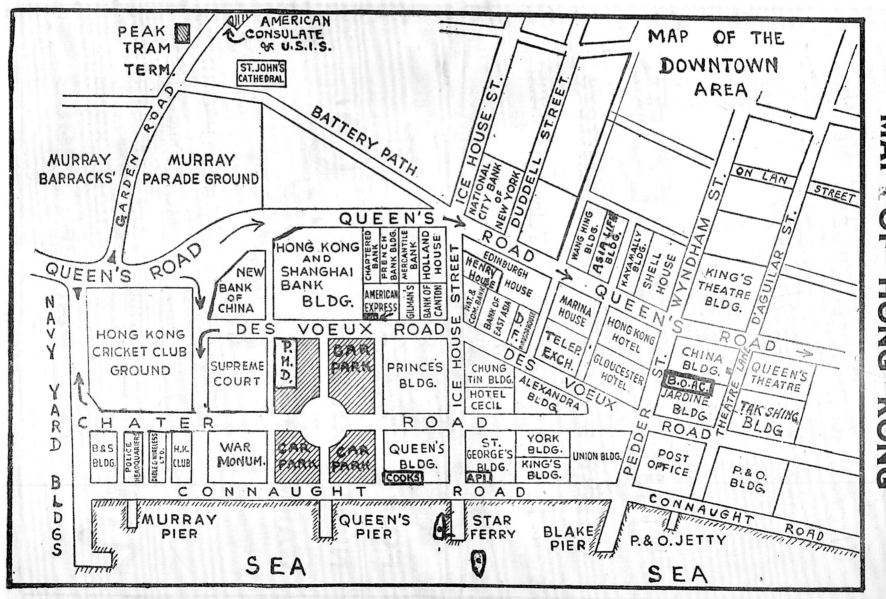

1.22

Approaching the ferry landing at Hong Kong, with rickshaws waiting for passengers in front of the King's Building. Summer 1948.

1.23

Royal or Statue Square with the HSBC and Prince's Buildings. The hills in the background forming the Peak district were frequently shrouded in clouds during the summer. Summer 1948.

Fishermen working with their nets along the Central Praya on Connaught Road. The Hong Kong Club, Queen's Building, General Post Office, P&O Building and Star Ferry pier are in the background. Summer 1948.

1.25

'A short way behind the plaza, Hong Kong Summer 1948.' A gas street lamp is here seen next to the Murray Parade Ground, with the HSBC building and Supreme Court (now the Court of Final Appeal) in the background.

1.26

'A basket of live chickens goes by three-wheeler bike, summer 1948'.

1.27

'Active woman laborer off to her home
after toiling at a construction project, road
building or street repair. Hong Kong,
Summer 1948.'

1.28

Next to the playground on Queen's Road East near the Royal Naval Yards at Wanchai, two girls talking loudly, with one of them chewing sugar cane.

1.29

'A Chinese girl with long pigtails, Hong Kong Summer 1948'.

1.30

The open-air Peak Café had just been transformed from the Peak Lookout in 1947. This photograph shows a view from the interior looking out over the South China Sea to the south of Hong Kong Island. Summer 1948.

1.31

Looking from the Peak across the Botanical Gardens and Central towards Kowloon and the distant mountains of the New Territories. Summer 1948.

1.32

Haw Par Mansion formed part of the Tiger Balm Estate on the hills above Causeway Bay. It was surrounded by a formal garden. This photograph, taken in the summer of 1948, shows the garden with its carefully trimmed lawns, but without the bonsai trees that were trained to grow in the shape of Chinese characters during the later period.

1.33

'Perhaps it was the grave of one of the wealthy brothers'. Tiger Balm Garden, Hong Kong, in the summer of 1948.

1.34

'More of Tiger Balm, Summer 1948'

1.35

'The Great Tiger Balm pagoda in the Tiger Balm Estate, now opened as a park to the public, Summer 1948.'

1.36

Haw Par Mansion at Tiger Balm Estate over-looking Victoria Harbour and the rocky hills above Kowloon. Summer 1948.

Another view of the palatial gardens and house built by two Chinese brothers, where a dozen or more German shepherd dogs were penned in a small yard at the back. Summer 1948.

1.38

A new tower of delicate porcelain workmanship nearing completion in the grounds of Tiger Balm Garden. Summer 1948.

Chapter 2

The visitors

A 1957 Hong Kong Government publication waxed lyrical about the attractions of Hong Kong to both businessmen and tourists from overseas:

'The attractions of Hong Kong need no introduction to the businessman who lives here, but may perhaps not be as well known to the overseas visitor and those businessmen visiting as tourists. Hong Kong has indeed a very special atmosphere, a blend of east and west, of bustle and peace, of relaxation and vitality, in a setting splendid enough to challenge comparison with any corner of the world celebrated for beauty or interest.

Anybody who steps out of an aeroplane after circling the harbour, anybody who has landed from a ship after slipping through the pass of Lei Yue Mun must experience that tingle of excitement which most of us who live here never quite lose. This quickened sense of expectation, familiar to visitors to New York or London, to Paris or Peking, will not be unjustified.

To the seasoned traveler, perhaps the special feeling of Hong Kong is its transparent unselfconsciousness. Its inhabitants are on the whole only dimly aware of their spectacular twin cities in which the goods of all the world are offered in a jolly hugger-mugger, vividly lit by a tropical sun during the day and by a million lights after dark. They take for granted the extraordinary cheek-by-jowl contrasts presented by great ships and junks, buicks and rickshaws, Chinese gowns and western suits, neon signs and joss sticks, temples and emporia, bamboo poles and lorries, black roof-tiles and concrete, electricity and wood smoke, gongs and 33 r.p.ms., gold and tinsel, paste and jade. Residents may take the funicular to the Peak only to get out of the town for a week-end walk with the family, but the visitor is unlikely to forget his journey up the Peak or the breath-taking vistas that it brings him from the upper terminus.

Hong Kong has few special attractions to offer other than itself. Only a fascinating, cosmopolitan, modern city, well swept, tidy and alive, imbued with the Chinese genius for zestful living, cheerfulness and hospitality, a shopper's paradise, set among towering hills on either side of a blue harbour. At night whether viewed from hilltop, street or ferry, an astonishing panorama of scintillating lights. Half an hour away among the windy hills and bays and islands, the immemorial life of rural China continues gently and unself-consciously. Half an hour away too, western leisure may be enjoyed on beach and golf course and at sea, in club-house, hotel, or restaurant.

Which man or woman has not visited Hong Kong's few square miles and does not hanker to be there again?[1]

This description of Hong Kong, written by an English journalist six decades ago, might almost have been written in the year 2018. It will certainly have a familiar ring for the visitor today. Though Hong Kong has undoubtedly kept abreast of the times during the intervening era, it cannot quite shake itself free of its image as a place where the modernity of the West meets the timelessness of the East. This feature fascinated tourists to the city throughout the post-war period.

1
Hong Kong Government, Directory of Commerce, Industry, Finance, 1957 (Hong Kong, 1957), p. 123.

2.1

A Cathay Pacific DC-4 aircraft ready for boarding on the apron at Kai Tak Airport during a winter in the 1950s.

2.2

By the 1950s, Cathay Pacific had already become the local airline that represented Hong Kong to the outside world. In July 1955, Cathay Pacific aircraft engineer Pappy Cowan finishes his work for the day, preparing the aircraft compartment for his own 'landing'.

2.3

As European and American travelers began to travel to Hong Kong by jet aeroplane in the 1960s, a new post-war era of mass tourism began. This photograph shows passengers on the tarmac of Kai Tak Airport in January 1965, preparing to leave the city on a Cathay Pacific flight.

2.4

Shirley MacLaine disembarking from a
British Overseas Airways Corporation
(B.O.A.C.) flight at Kai Tak Airport in 1956
after playing Princess Aouda in the movie
'Around the World in 80 Days'.

2.5
A BOAC bus waiting for the arrival of
passengers at Kai Tak Airport in the 1950s.

2.6

Passengers board a chain of shuttle buses at Kai Tak Airport during a winter in the 1950s.

2.7

People awaiting the arrival of friends and relatives near the temporary arrivals hall at Kai Tak Airport in the 1950s. Construction workers are taking a break after removing the old wooden fence and replacing it with metal mesh wire fence. The airport control tower can be seen in the background.

2.8

Beauties in the air

In the 1950s and 1960s, working as a flight attendant was a glamorous career, with only the most outstanding women chosen to work in the air. Selected for their good figures and friendly demeanour, their jobs were actually quite demanding. This photograph shows an air hostess at Kai Tak Airport in 1958. She is wearing a white cheongsam, which was considered to be eminetly appropriate as a smart airline uniform.

2.9

In the 1960s, British and American warships often docked in Hong Kong, which served as a refueling and maintenance centre in the South China Sea. In this unusual photograph taken in Victoria Harbour on 14 May 1966, two US submarines are berthed side by side. Sailors are ready to board a 'walla-walla' boat for their sightseeing tour on land.

2.10

The Peninsula Hotel was the most luxurious hotel in Hong Kong in the 1950s and 1960s, with 322 splendidly appointed rooms. 'The Pen' was the top choice of politicians, celebrities and wealthy visitors from around the world. This photograph shows delighted American guests with smartly-dressed bellboys at the entrance of the hotel in November 1964.

2.11

A group of American soldiers equipped with cameras at the ready gather outside the Shamrock Hotel on Nathan Road in the 1950s. Most visitors would stay at medium-class hotels in Tsimshatsui or Wanchai. A single bedroom at the Shamrock Hotel in 1967 cost US$20-$35 per day, while the Peninsula charged US$90-$150.

2.12 & 2.13

Tsimshatsui was the hub of rickshaws. These two photographs show a couple of well-dressed western ladies taking rickshaw journeys outside the KCR railway terminus in the early 1960s. A red Royal Mail lorry with distinctive Hong Kong number plates is parked outside ready to collect mail.

2.14

During the peak tourist season in July 1961, rickshaws carrying western tourists are parked temporarily near the car park at the junction of Salisbury and Nathan Roads in Tsimshatsui. Taking a picture with the rickshaw pullers was a favourite activity for tourists. This massive outdoor car park of 450,0000 square feet opposite the Peninsula Hotel was sold in 1969 for a record-breaking HK$130 million (or $2,661 per square foot), six times higher than the reserve price. The five-star Sheraton Hotel, 17 storeys high and with 1,100 rooms above a shopping mall, was constructed on the site in the early 1970s.

2.15

This photograph, taken in October 1964, show a businessman carrying a bag from the Ambassador Hotel. He seems to be lost in the streets outside the Emba Mink House at 31A Carnarvon Road. The 'danger' warning sign was placed on the street because of an underground cabling project conducted by Hong Kong Telephone Company. This was a time of rapid development for the Hong Kong telephone network.

2.16

A gentleman took this picture at the junction of Carnarvon Road and Bristol Avenue in late 1949 or early 1950 when the Grand Hotel had just opened. A well-dressed lady is holding tightly to her camera on a rickshaw, ready to shoot tourist photographs in the area.

2.17

A Citytourama tour guide is seen here unloading tourists from a van on the roadside on their way to Aberdeen in 1963.

2.18

A western lady seems to be very interested in the dry fish market at Central on a winter's day during the 1950s.

2.19 & 2.20

Tour escort companies came into operation in the post-war period. Tourist guides who could speak English had well-paid jobs. This photograph shows an elegantly dressed lady called Ying Ying, who was a privately-employed tour guide. She brought tourists from International Hotel in Cameron Road to visit Garden House (known as Garden Mansion today) next to St Mary's Canossian College in Austin Road, Tsimshatsui in July 1955. The tourist took a picture of Ying Ying at the entrance to the House.

2.21

Hello! How are you?

Aberdeen was not only a fishing village but also an important tourist destination. This photograph was taken at the No. 7 bus route terminal at Aberdeen in the 1950s. A Western tourist is greeting a child wandering along the street in bare feet. In the background is the Sang Kong Restaurant, serving Cantonese seafood. On the right, is the entrance to the Tai Pak Floating Restaurant.

2.22

Beauty by the shore

A sweet and immaculately dressed boat girl photographed together with American sailors at Aberdeen in the 1950s. After taking the photograph, whether the sailors understood her or not, she would shout with her Tanka accent, 'Sir, if you want to take a boat tour, please come to mine!'

2.23

Visitors to Hong Kong did not necessarily come just for sightseeing. Some came on special study tours to investigate the public housing schemes of the Hong Kong government. This photograph shows a group of westerners being escorted by Hong Kong government officials inspecting the Shek Kei Mei resettlement estate in January 1963.

2.24

Lascar Row in Sheung Wan contained a sprawling market during the 1950s and 1960s selling all manner of antiquities from different Chinese dynasties. Tourists would come here treasure hunting. This photograph shows a group of westerners with their Chinese guide looking for curios to take back home with them. However, some seem to be more interested in the tenement buildings and crowded living conditions in Hong Kong.

2.25 & 2.26

There were a few tourist companies set up in the 1950s and 1960s which employed professional tour guides with specialist training who could speak various foreign languages. These photographs taken in March 1967 show an attractive female tour guide dressed in uniform, at Tiger Balm Garden where she is escorting Japanese tourists.

2.27

Tiger Balm Garden was the most important of Hong Kong's post-war tourist sights. Tourist information at that time would always introduce the Garden as a 'must visit place', so it attracted all sorts of visitors including local residents and foreign naval personnel, as shown in this photograph taken in the 1960s.

2.28

Among the various exhibits at Tiger Balm Garden, there were many educational scenes demonstrating the importance of filial piety. This photograph of a western visitor escorted by a Chinese lady holding a colourful umbrella was taken on 13 November 1963 in front of statues representing the importance of filial piety.

2.29

Seeing the 'Bamboo Curtain' separating
Mainland China from Hong Kong was a
thrilling visit for Western tourists in the
1960s. The best way to see 'Red China'
from Hong Kong was across the Shenzhen
River from the hill at Lok Ma Chau Police
Station. This photograph shows western
gentlemen in a rented car uncovering
'the secrets of the Mainland' in 1963. The
local villagers were also a great attraction
wearing their traditional dress.

2.30

Another photograph taken in June 1962 shows a western lady on a trip to the boundary 'Closed Area', being photographed with a group of villagers in front of an eye-catching Police Department warning board.

Chapter 3

City sights

Overlooking its magnificent harbour, the City of Victoria extends along the shore for nearly four miles and rises from the water's edge to an elevation of more than six hundred feet. Nearest to the harbour are the banks, offices, shops and godowns – many built upon land reclaimed from the harbour; further up are the serried rows of houses in the Mid-Levels, resting on their massive terraces; and all along the Peak are the mansions of the wealthy, perched along the skyline where the summer temperatures are appreciably lower.

On the waterfront, the eye is perhaps first drawn towards the Royal Naval Dockyard, with its huge crane and moored warships. A little to the west, Statue Square is the broad civic space where Hong Kong's most impressive buildings and notable memorials stand: the beautiful Supreme Court; the HSBC Hong Kong headquarters; the Queen's Building; the Cenotaph; the handsome offices of shipping firms. Tourists are advised to idle along the busy waterfront where steamers, junks and smaller craft jostle each other for space. Here you will note the contrasts offered by the passing throng – Chinese, Europeans, Indians, Japanese – study their varied costumes, hear their many tongues. One should not miss the tram ride from Des Voeux Road and through Wanchai, the Eastern Chinese quarter, to Happy Valley, where Hong Kong's famous racecourse is situated, and along the hillside the various cemeteries – Anglican, Roman Catholic, Mohammedan, Parsee and Hindu, all reconfirming the polyglot status of Hong Kong throughout the last century.

Walking into the oldest streets of Hong Kong along Queen's Road Central, you notice that Hong Kong has miles of shops. Shops for clothing, coffins, crockery, blackwood furniture, cameras, rattan work, curios, jewelry, silk clothing, drugs, fortune-telling and refreshments. There are shops catering mainly for locals with pickled delicacies made from vegetables or snakes; Chinese herbal shops; barber shops; pawnshops; dentist shops and beauty parlours. Cat Street offers hardware products from doorknobs to gold watches, antiques from porcelain to fine furniture; and in the covered markets there are stalls for vegetables, fish, shark's fin and other aromatic delicacies. In the Chinese-populated Western district, verandahs overhang the footpaths, with shop signs and clothes-props cluttering the sides of the buildings so that the streets appear to be much narrower even than they are. Crowds flock into the narrow streets day and night, and there is much good-tempered jostling and confusion – especially at the cross-roads.

Everyone takes in Kowloon as part of their Hong Kong tour. The entire Kowloon Peninsula is well planned, its original hilly spine having been tamed by the promethean might of colonial government and private developers into a bustling urban space through the demolition of whole hills and the reclamation of large areas of the foreshore. Kowloon is part of 'the Mainland' (according to observations by early visitors); it extends from Tsimshatsui along a straight two-mile run through Kowloon's principal thoroughfare – Nathan Road. The tip of Tsimshatsui boasts Kowloon's most striking landmarks: the Kowloon-Canton railway station, the adjacent Star Ferry Pier. Looking east from the railway station, the eye quickly notes the grand Peninsula Hotel. Further along the peninsula are the wharves where the big Pacific liners berth.

Most tourists visiting Kowloon do not venture any further along Nathan Road than Yau Ma Tei. Their focus is on Tsimshatsui, the shop window of Hong Kong. There you will find huge buildings and crowded tenements. Here are the magnificent hotels and a bewildering array of street-food stalls. Shops sell everything that the tourist wants – curios, jewelry, cameras, and clothes. Here you will find all these products concentrated in one place, much more convenient for the shopper than anywhere on Hong Kong Island. There are high-priced curios and porcelains, pearls and diamonds, but only the expert can tell what is real and what is fake. Tsimshatsui is the melting pot of Hong Kong's diverse population. Here on the street you can meet all races and creeds, and all classes of people – business people, wealthy ladies, gentlemen, rich merchants, working men and women, teddy boys and attractive girls in brightly-coloured cheongsams – all of which suggests that Hong Kong is one of the most cosmopolitan places in the world.

When you have seen all the city's sights and felt Hong Kong's sense of Western grandeur and Eastern glamour (the grandeur of achievement and the glamour of oriental life); when you have weighed the future's magnificent promise, noting the vast development projects in progress which seem to be literally moving mountains and reclaiming the waterfront; you may be able to grasp in some measure the complex and bewitching nature of a city that is hailed as one of the most interesting ports of call, and one of the most fascinating places to call 'home' in the whole wide world.

3.1 (Previous page) & 3.2

Taking the ferry in December 1958, one would pass these pre-war pai laus (rows of tenement houses) along the Sheung Wan and Sai Ying Pun waterfronts. Their lower floors were used as warehouses for the import and export of South East Asian foodstuffs, and offices for overseas traders.

3.3

The older Star ferries of the 1950s still retained their high chimney stacks and the sleek lines that were reminiscent of Shanghai ferries during the Republican era. A ferry journey on the upper deck (first class) across the harbour would cost 20 cents, half price on the lower deck.

3.4

After the second phase of reclamation in
Central, a new twin-pier Star Ferry terminal
and clock tower was completed in 1957.
This photograph was taken soon after the
new Star Ferry Pier came into service.

The first phase of post-war reclamation on Hong Kong Island, from Murray Road to the original site of the Star Ferry pier, was completed in 1954, resulting in an area of around 388,000 square feet being added to the waterfront. Queen's Pier and City Hall were constructed on this new site. This photograph was taken in the mid-1950s and shows the newly reclaimed land. In the middle distance is the financial centre of Hong Kong with the prominent Bank of China and HSBC Buildings. In the foreground are Prince's and Queen's Buildings to the left and the Supreme Court to the right of the HSBC bank – the 'Azure Dragon' and 'White Tiger'.

3.6

The imposing granite façade of the HSBC building taken from Statue Square in the late 1950s. Statue Square was converted from the pre-war civic garden into a carpark in the late-1940s.

3.7

This 1950s photograph shows the new Bank of China Building and the 1930s HSBC Building. Both were financial institutions that had been established in Hong Kong for many decades. As time passed, the roles played by these two banks in the city waxed and waned.

The second-generation Hong Kong Club Building was constructed in 1897 on reclaimed land next to Chater Road, Central. When the building was first completed and for decades afterwards, it was photographed in black-and-white, but these original photographs were often over-painted with a light wash of watercolour. This brightly coloured photograph of the building was taken on 12 July 1965. The thousands of surviving images of the Hong Kong Club Building bear witnesses to the development of photography in Hong Kong – from black-and-white in the late nineteenth century to glossy colour images in the mid-twentieth century. The building was demolished in 1981 amid much controversy to make way for a new clubhouse and office tower.

3.9

The old Supreme Court in Central (now the Court of Final Appeal) has been a symbol of the rule of law in Hong Kong and an iconic landmark for more than one hundred years. By the early 1960s, after the Central reclamation, part of the post-war outdoor car park had been redesignated as a small park. In order to prevent construction of new buildings in front of its headquarters, HSBC had purchased this plot of land during the 1890s reclamation project to avoid the site's feng shui being spoiled.

3.10

The new City Hall, built in the Bauhaus architectural style, began operation on 2 March 1962. The construction cost was HK$20 million. This photograph was taken in September 1960, showing the completed Star Ferry carpark with the City Hall High Block to the right still under construction.

3.11

The American Consulate building on
Garden Road in September 1963.

3.12

Government House in the 1950s. Completely remodeled by the Japanese during the war years, this historic building has not changed very much in the intervening decades.

3.13

The entrance to Government House is being guarded in the 1950s by two British soldiers and two stone lions.

3.14

The Botanic Gardens in the early 1950s,
with the Mid-Levels and Peak district rising
in the background.

3.15

The Vehicular Ferry Pier in Central was established in 1933 near Jubilee Street. Bus route No. 7 was the public transport route of choice for those heading to the western parts of Hong Kong Island and Aberdeen. The route went from Central to Aberdeen via Connaught Road Central, Connaught Road West, Eastern Street, Queen's Road Central, Pokfulam Road, and through to Aberdeen. Buses came every 15 to 20 minutes on average, with different charges for sections of the journey. Bus fares ranged from 10 cents to 20 cents, making this form of transport particularly popular with working class people. Taken in September 1960, this photograph shows rickshaws that were used for transporting small goods, very different from rickshaws in Tsimshatsui and Kowloon that were mainly used by tourists.

3.16

Tram avenue

The tramway outside the Gloucester Hotel and Jardine's building (later replaced by Wheelock House) on Des Voeux Road Central. On the right is the General Post Office. Travelling by tram was the cheapest and most enjoyable form of transport, allowing the passenger to see the whole north side of the Island in one journey. Once onboard the top deck of a tram in Des Voeux Road Central, you would travel slowly through crowded streets all the way to Shau Kei Wan, at the eastern end of the Island, at a cost of 20 cents.

3.17

This photograph was taken in July 1955 outside the President Line offices in the St George's Building, Connaught Road Central. This bustling area was always extremely busy and lively.

3.18

The Financial Centre

This photograph captures the streets of the financial district of Central in September 1960, taken from outside the Hong Kong and Shanghai Bank. The tall building in the centre is the Bank of East Asia Building, next to the United Chinese Bank Building (now New Henry House). To the right is the old Prince's Building.

3.19

A photograph taken outside the Chartered Bank with a view along Queen's Road Central to the west in the 1950s. The newly completed York House is on the right.

3.20

The busiest area in the Central district was the junction between Queen's Road Central and Wyndham Street. This photograph, taken in the 1950s, shows the King's Theatre with an advertisement for 'The Sign of the Cross', an old Cecil B. DeMille movie from 1932.

3.21

A 1950s view looking up D'Aguilar Street
outside the King's Theatre. The New World
Café was located at the junction of Stanley
Street, opposite the Practical Book Store.

3.22

A view of On Lan Street from the junction
of Wyndham Street where silk, linen lace
and handkerchiefs retail and wholesale
business were located in the 1950s.

3.23

Crowds bustling across the road at the junction of Jubilee Street and Queen's Road Central. In the 1950s, people carried paper bags or wrapped their goods in newspaper, at a time when no-one talked about environmental protection. Plastic was a new and expensive material, and would not be used for wrapping food for several decades.

3.24

Further along Queen's Road in 1961, more shops for locals could be found selling Chinese medicine, Shanghainese food and roasted pork, among other daily necessities.

3.25

Queen's Road was the first road constructed in Hong Kong during early colonial times, connecting the east with the west. It was later divided into the central, eastern and western sections. Queen's Road Central ran through the oldest commercial area. In the 1950s and 1960s, there were still a number of pre-war tenement houses on both sides of the road, covered in older-style signboards and some of the newer neon signs. In this photograph, taken in September 1960, the Man Hing Drug Company at 277 Queen's Road Central can be clearly seen. Among the various shops, only the feng shui shop of Choi Park-Lai at 265 Queen's Road Central and the Central flagship store of Lee Kum Kee Oyster Sauce at 262 Queen's Road Central still exist today.

3.26

Jewelry shops on Queen's Road Central. The Tai Shun Jewelry & Goldsmith shop and the Yam Ling Kee Jewelry shop were located at 270A & B Queen's Road Central. This photograph was taken in November 1967.

3.27

Pottinger Street, also called Ladder Street, is one of the oldest streets in the central district of Hong Kong. Named after the first governor of Hong Kong, this photograph was taken from Stanley Street in the 1950s.

3.28

Jervois Street after the rain

The narrow streets and lanes in the older areas of Central were a distinctive feature of Hong Kong Island. Among them, Jervois Street was a hub for traditional Chinese shops. Were it not for She Wong Lam snake cuisine at 90 Jervois Street and Luk Kee Cheong Hardware Store located at the junction of 38 Hillier Street, it would be difficult to identify precisely the location of this street view dated September 1960.

3.29

This photograph, also dated September 1960, was taken in Jervois Street, still full of traditional shops and Chinese medicine clinics. Among them, Sanyang Trading Company at 33 Jervois Street, Mei Lee Long Grocery, and the Chen Zhi-yun Chinese medicine clinic were all established to serve locals in the area.

3.30

A snap shot of street activities at the junction of Tai Ping Shan Street towards Po Yan Street in the 1950s.

3.31

An earlier photograph of Circular Pathway taken in September 1960. The narrow lane at the end of Upper Lascar Row and overshadowed by a massive stone retaining wall on the right, was the hub of paper product supplies on the Island in the 1960s. Hillier Street was just around the corner. The close-packed tenements with washing hanging on the verandahs indicate how crowded the environment was for residents.

3.32

The photograph shows Circular Pathway in the Taipingshan area of Central in March 1964. Among the small-scale family-operated industrial shops to be found in this part of Hong Kong Island were Tung Tai Paper Box at 17 Circular Pathway, Sun Hing Stationery and Paperboard at 19 Circular Pathway, and On Long Gold and Silvery Jewelry at 20 Circular Pathway.

3.33

A view of Upper Lascar Row from Lok Ku Road taken in September 1960. The shop located at this prominent spot was Yue Po Chai Chinese Curios which survives to this day, although now relocated to a bigger shop next to the Man Mo Temple.

3.34

National Treasure Hunt

Antique shops in Hong Kong mainly sold artefacts of Chinese porcelain, glass, gold, silver, bronze and other materials, many of which had been brought out of China in the late 1940s and early 1950s. Expatriate civil servants working in the Hong Kong government and short-stay businessmen would hunt for treasures in these well-known curio shops. When these people retired from Hong Kong, their Chinese antiquities would be taken back to their hometowns across the world, and in this way many treasures were eventually sold or auctioned at a considerable profit. This photograph was taken in September 1960, showing a selection of curios being sold at that time.

3.35

Old tenement houses near Yan Woo Restaurant at 138 Hollywood Road under renovation in October 1965. Hollywood Road was named by Sir John Francis Davis, the second Governor of Hong Kong, after his home town near Bristol, England in 1845.

3.36

A grand opening floral display outside the Shan Chuen Tea House on Hollywood Road in September 1960.

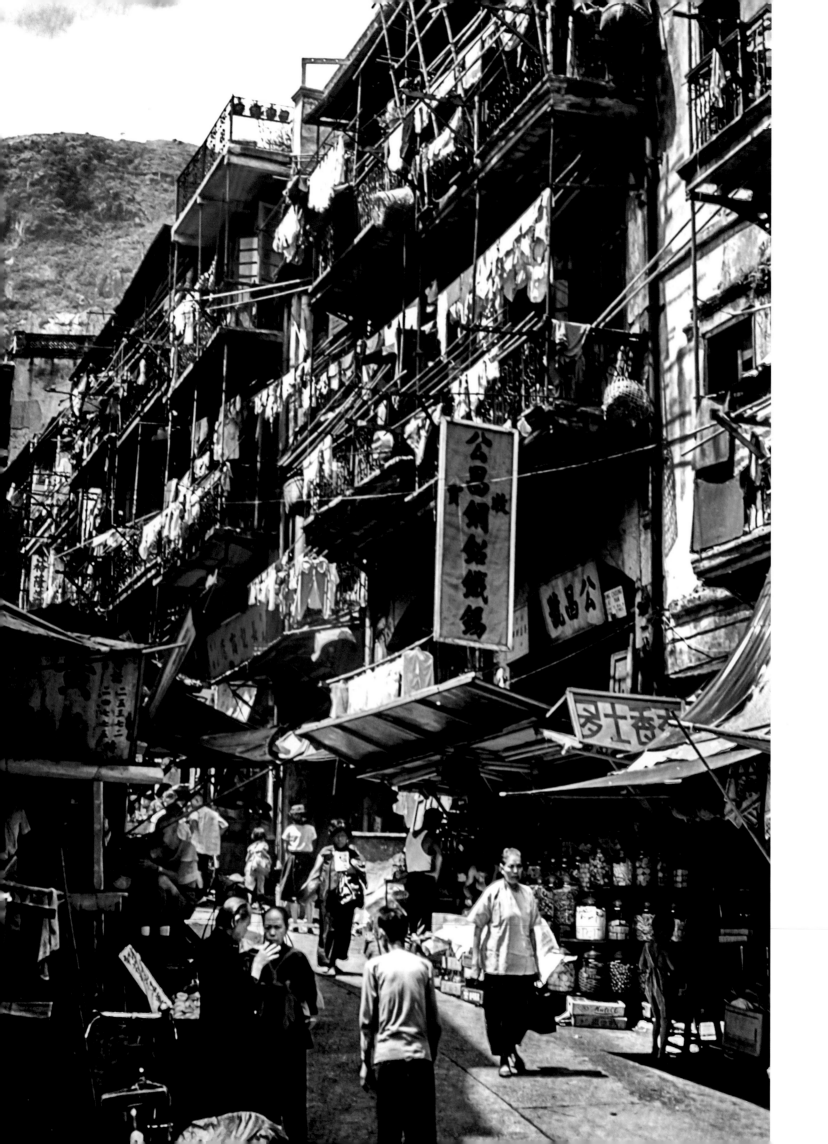

3.37

Elgin Street

This photograph shows tenement houses on Elgin Street, Hong Kong Island in September 1960. Kung Cheung Ho, situated at the street junction here, bought scrap copper and iron from customers.

3.38

The praya along Gloucester Road, Wanchai, was a busy dockside loading area from the 1930s. In this 1959 photograph, a Mobil marine diesel station can be seen to the far right, while the tallest building along this stretch of the praya is the Luk Kwok Hotel.

3.39

A road sign for Queen's Road East taken near the Wanchai Market in December 1958.

3.40

A busy street scene in November 1966 on Johnston Road in Wanchai, where there were many big Chinese restaurants cheek-by-jowl with department stores selling produce from the Mainland.

3.41

An old tenement building with open balconies adjacent to the Luk Kwok Hotel on Jaffe Road in November 1966. A sign for Luk Kwok Bridal arrangement service can be seen on the corner of the building.

3.42

St. Mary's Church (Episcopal) located at Tung Lo Wan Road in the Tai Hang area was built in 1937 but only recommenced its services after the war in 1949. This photograph, taken in the 1950s, shows the Western interpretation of Chinese architecture typical of the 1920s and 1930s in Hong Kong.

3.43

A view of Hennessy Road from the junction of Jardine's Bazaar. The recently-opened New York Theatre was situated at the corner of Percival Road in this 1955 photograph. The buildings along this stretch of tramway were later redeveloped as the East Point Centre and Sogo Department Store.

3.44

A bird's eye view of the Happy Valley
racecourse with Jardine's Lookout behind
in December 1964.

3.45

A view of the Mid-Levels and Sheung Wan district from Bonham Road in the 1950s. Ling Kwong Middle School, painted in white to the left, was located at 10 Po Hing Fong.

3.46

Haw Par Mansion was caught between two very different worlds and is a prime example of the 'Chinese Renaissance' style of architecture that mixes oriental and Western features. French doors with delicate stained-glass moon windows depicting birds and bamboo lead into rooms elaborately furnished with art deco mirrors from Belgium, carved wooden bears from Switzerland, Italian marble nymphs and an early Ferranti electric grandfather clock. This photograph was taken in the 1950s.

3.47

This popular Tiger Balm Garden exhibit from the 1950s shows a washroom scene featuring Kwai Fei, the Tang Dynasty beauty.

3.48

A harbour view taken from a wharf near Causeway Bay looking towards Tsimshatsui in March 1961. Coolies are busy unloading baskets from a boat.

3.49

The lavatory at the Star Ferry pier in Kowloon was a popular place for tourists and locals. In September 1960 it also had one of the best views of the harbour.

3.50

This photograph was taken in October 1960 at the Salisbury Road entrance of the Peninsula Hotel. A line of bright red rickshaws are queuing on the road, awaiting custom from tourists staying at the hotel. The official fare for riding rickshaws was 50 cents for every five minutes. The government stopped issuing licences for rickshaws in 1968, and by 1970 there were only 170 rickshaws left in the colony.

3.51

Famous among Mainland Chinese tourists today, Canton Road has become a major shopping avenue in Hong Kong. This image of Canton Road in June 1962 shows it was already a major tourist attraction at that time. The only difference is that it was previously frequented by European and American tourists. Shops included Dairy Farm at 28 Canton Road, selling milk and ice cream. Rickshaws, which could be seen everywhere in Tsimshatsui, are parked on the roadside awaiting customers.

3.52

Mody Road in Tsimshatsui, in March 1967. On the right is Ocean View Court, the commercial and residential building facing Chatham Road that had recently been completed by Kiu Fung Construction Company.

3.53

Chevrolet Impala

The new model Chevrolet Impala of US General Motors was introduced into Hong Kong in the 1950s when the automobile import market was rapidly developing. This photograph, taken at the junction of Mody Road and Nathan Road in Tsimshatsui in August 1958, shows a new Chevrolet Impala 1958 parked outside the China Radio & Electrical Company's shop. Its appealing dual-tone appearance attracted a passing tourist to snap some pictures. Note the signboard of the Thomson Shoe Company in the upper left corner of the photograph. The shop was located at 225 Nathan Road.

3.54

An early colour photograph taken at the junction of Nathan Road and Carnarvon Road in late 1949 or early 1950, when the Grand Hotel was still being prepared for its grand opening.

3.55

The most powerful storm of the 1960s, Typhoon Marie, struck Hong Kong on the night of 7 and 8 June 1960. Many downtown districts of Hong Kong Island and the Kowloon Peninsula were devastated by her destructive power. This photograph shows the post-typhoon debris from fallen trees outside the Grand Hotel (established in 1950) in Carnarvon Road, Tsim Sha Tsui. Many vehicles parked on the roadside were seriously damaged in this storm.

3.56

Tsimshatsui was a maze of intertwined streets which many tourists found difficult to navigate. Along Cameron Road, photographed here in August 1958, all the shops were designed to appeal to tourists, with English signs and numerous Western clothing and camera shops. Seeing the harbour in the distance near Chatham Road was one way that the tourists could work out where they were.

3.57

Humphreys Avenue

The business and film processing departments of the Kowloon branch of Asia Photo Supply Limited were located at 2A Humphreys Avenue, Tsimshatsui, in 1959. The end of the street runs into Nathan Road near its junction with Haiphong Road.

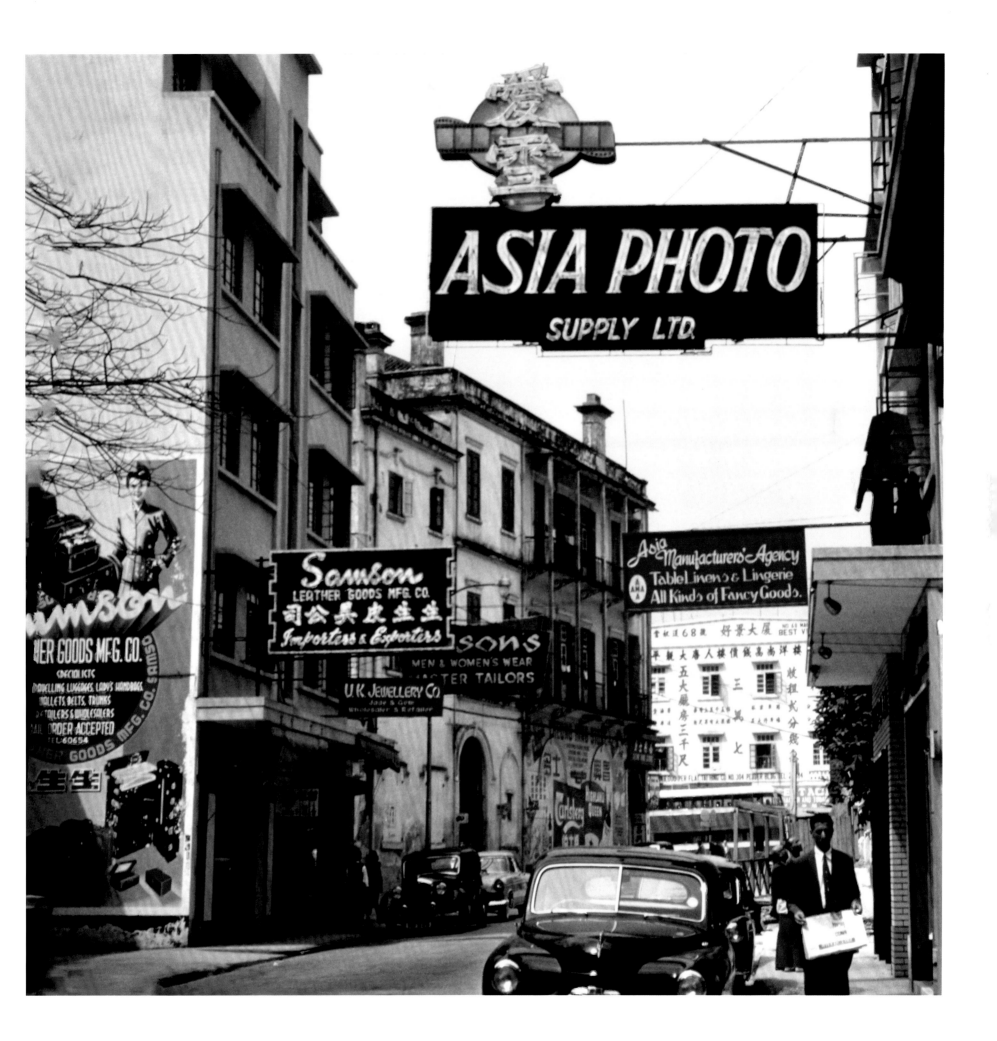

3.58

Haiphong Road, Tsimshatsui

The junction of Nathan Road and Haiphong Road, Tsimshatsui, in December 1958. The trees on the right led to the entrance to Whitfield Barracks (today's Kowloon Park). Haiphong Mansion on the left was a crowded tenement building with residents living in small subdivided flats. Drying poles extend from balconies over the street below on washing day. The lifestyle in these dilapidated tenement buildings was portrayed in the popular 1973 Shaw Brothers movie 'The House of 72 Tenants'.

3.59

Little Shanghai

Many Shanghainese restaurants had already been established in Granville Road, Tsimshatsui, by July 1962 when this photograph was taken. Many Shanghainese had moved to Hong Kong after the conclusion of the Chinese Civil War in 1949, with quite a few of them settling down in Tsimshatsui, including Du Yue-Sheng, the leader of the biggest Shanghai Triad gang.

3.60

There are a substantial number of companies and businesses that have been established in Hong Kong for more than fifty years. Among these is the Four Seas China Silk Company in Tak Shing Street, off Nathan Road. This photograph shows the original shop in July 1955, where Four Seas Mansion is currently located.

3.61

Nathan Road, named after Sir Matthew Nathan, the thirteenth governor of Hong Kong (1904-7), is a wide avenue that cuts through the Kowloon Peninsula from Victoria Harbour to Boundary Street, the pre-1898 border with China. In this photograph dated July 1955 the section of Nathan Road between Austin Road and Jordan Road can be seen, with its big department stores selling daily necessities, clothes and shoes.

3.62

Mongkok Ferry Terminal in September 1960.

3.63

A traffic policeman on duty in Castle Peak
Road, Shek Kip Mei, where the Golden
Gate Bakery No.1 shop was located in
July 1962.

3.64

Lai Yuen Amusement Park was one of the most popular entertainment venues for the people of Hong Kong. The large red Chinese characters spell out 'Kung Hei Fat Choy' at the entrance during the Lunar New Year in February 1966.

3.65

Kat Hing Wai walled village in the days when its defensive moat was filled with water. This photograph taken in the 1950s shows the village walls reflected in the murky waters of the moat.

3.66

Taken in the northern part of New Territories in October 1962, this photograph shows ponds and hydroponic farmland; paddy rice fields are everywhere. Agriculture was still one of the key industries in Hong Kong at the beginning of the 1960s.

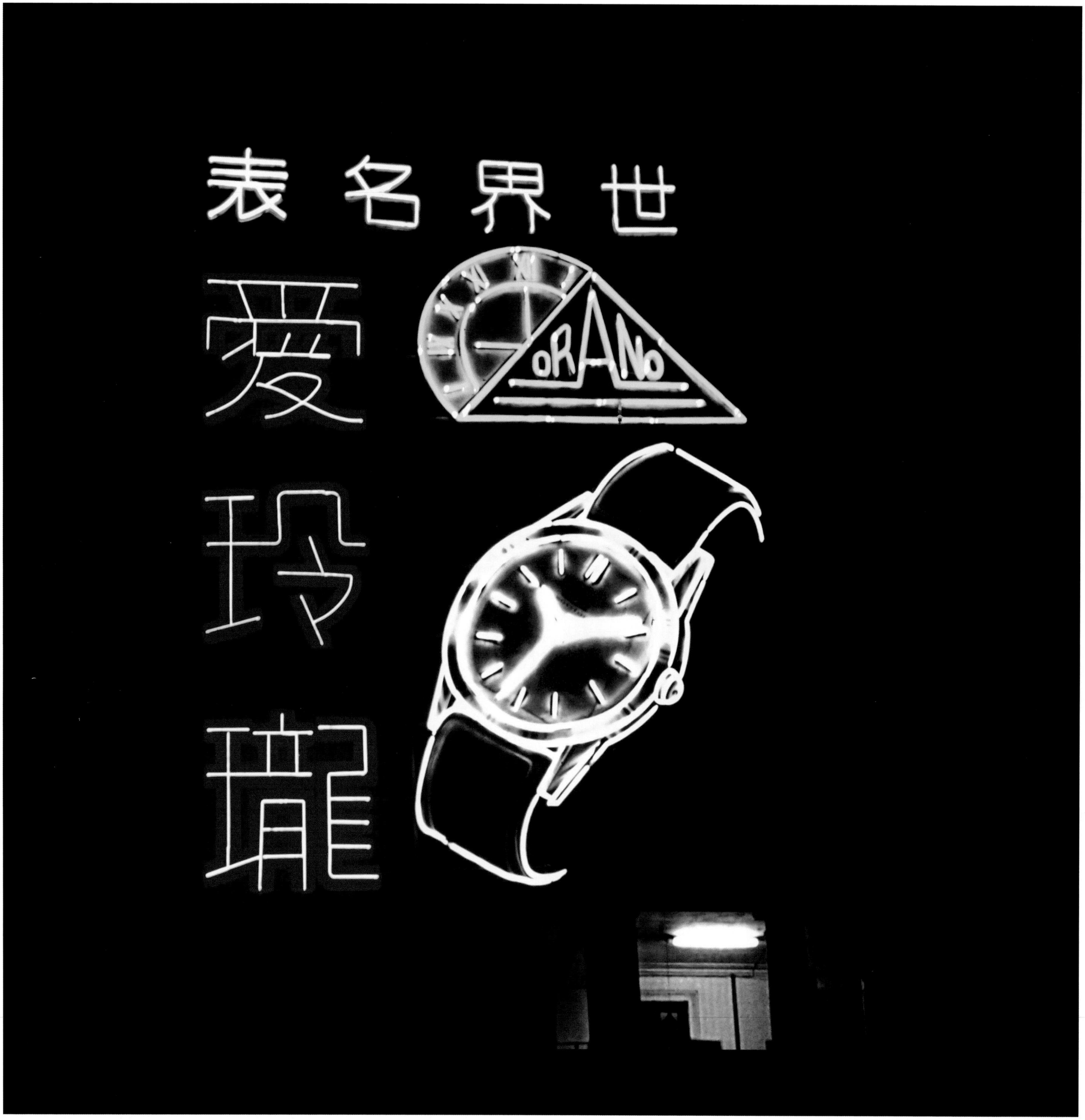
世界名表
oRANo
爱玲瓏

3.67

Night-time views of Hong Kong became world-renowned icons, with colourful Chinese neon billboards being instantly recognized features of the metropolitan districts. This neon billboard advertising 'the world famous watch brand Orano' photographed in September 1960 is very eye-catching.

3.68

Bright neon lighting was a crucial component of night-time photographs of Hong Kong and Kowloon. King Wah Restaurant at 620-628 Nathan Road, Kowloon, was both a large-scale Chinese restaurant and a nightclub. These neon lights in September 1960 guided tourists to their evening meal and post-prandial entertainment.

Chapter 4

The Peak

The most readily accessible vantage point for a panoramic view of Hong Kong is undoubtedly Victoria Peak. The Peak is itself a prominent landmark when viewed from the harbour, and one of the attractions of a Star Ferry ride has always been the view of Hong Kong Island with the Peak towering majestically above the city of Victoria. Once a tourist had landed on the Island, the Peak Tram funicular railway was the best choice for reaching the Peak. The cost of this trip was 60 cents in the 1950s, with the ascent to the top – 1,305 feet above sea level – being made in less than ten minutes. The experience of riding the Peak Tram is rather terrifying for some people, with an incline of 45 degrees in some places. Buildings along the route appear to lean at crazy angles. When the Peak itself comes into view, the houses clinging to the rocky outcrops seem almost to be on the point of falling away from the hillside. Everything about the Peak seems to defy the laws of gravity.

Once the intrepid tourist stepped out of the tram, the cool and bracing atmosphere of the Peak was immediately apparent, in stark contrast to the hot and stuffy city streets. The view from the Peak Tower was breath-taking. Commanding a 360-degree panorama of Hong Kong, the northern view encompassed the whole city, the bustling harbour, Kowloon and the New Territories, and on the southern side, the junks and fishing community of Aberdeen and the many outlying islands set like emeralds and black jade in the cerulean waters of the South China Sea. Below the Peak, you could see the busy harbour with ships of all nations. There were many impressive buildings which made Hong Kong one of the finest cities in East Asia: the HSBC building and the Bank of China building, but the tallest was the newer Alexandra House constructed in the early 1950s. The old Supreme Court and Hong Kong Club in their dignified civic settings made the panorama of Hong Kong complete, but modern apartments and luxury hotels were also beginning to rise from building sites across the city by the early 1960s. Ferries sketched a faint path across to Kowloon, where the clock tower of KCR terminus could be seen on the water-front with the YMCA, Peninsula Hotel and Signal Hill to its right. The

Royal Observatory mast was a prominent landmark, and in the background was the Nine Dragon Range, with Lion Rock at its centre, still clearly visible from the Peak in the days before air pollution. Kowloon City appeared as a dark smudge among the foothills at the head of its bay, while Tai Mo Shan, the highest peak in Hong Kong at 3,130 feet above sea level, was always visible on a clear day. Looking eastwards from the Peak towards Lei Yue Mun Pass the eye followed the graceful sweep of the Wanchai reclaimed area to Causeway Bay, Happy Valley and North Point; and westwards towards Green Island, Lantau and the coastline of the New Territories. The noises of the city drifted up to Lugard Road with surprising clarity.

Lugard Road encircles the Peak, so by strolling around towards the south, the energetic tourist could find the most charming views in Hong Kong: islands stretching away to the horizon on a broad expanse of blue water. Among the outlying islands, Cheung Chau could be easily recognized. It made a particularly arresting spectacle as the sun was setting, or before stormy weather, when the skies in Hong Kong are fantastic in their colours and dramatic movement. Upon reaching the south side of the Peak, tourists felt that they were in another world: not a silent world by any means, but rather than traffic and city noises assaulting the senses, these sounds emanated from rustling grass and fidgeting crickets, those curious insects that wind themselves up like a five-dollar watch and then let the mechanism run down with a buzz. Lugard Road gently undulates up and down the contours, with hidden glow-worms gleaming in the undergrowth.

The visitor to the Peak looked around in wonder at the buildings clinging to the hills, the roads cut through the rock or skirting precipitous slopes, the elaborate network of nullahs and drains running down to the harbour, the catchwaters and the reservoirs, and the extensive areas reclaimed from the sea .... an unforgettable view of Hong Kong.

4.1

The view of the Peak through the window
of Peninsula Hotel is clear and inviting in
September 1963.

4.2

The Star Ferry crosses the harbour in less than ten minutes from Kowloon to the Central praya on Hong Kong Island, back and forth, twenty hours a day. This photograph was taken on 12 July 1965

4.3

The tramway, which starts from Garden Road (100 feet above sea level), climbs rapidly to the Victoria Peak terminus some 1,305 feet above sea level. It is reputed to be the steepest funicular railway in the world and uses steel-wire cables to haul the tramcars. This photograph was taken in March 1961.

4.4

The Peak Tram on Hong Kong Island was built in the late nineteenth century for the wealthy expatriates who resided on the Peak. In the 1950s, the Peak Tram continued to serve the residents of the Peak, but it also became a popular tourist treat. The fare from Central to the peak was 60 cents. In this photograph, the tramcar is slowly approaching the Peak station.

In July 1955, both old and new buildings could be seen in the urban landscape on Hong Kong Island and alongside Victoria Harbour. In the Mid-Levels, older colonial buildings were retained until the 1960s, and Wanchai was also full of pre-war tenement houses. The most iconic buildings were the old HSBC Building and the Bank of China Building, but the Royal Navy base at Tamar was also quite prominent in its central position.

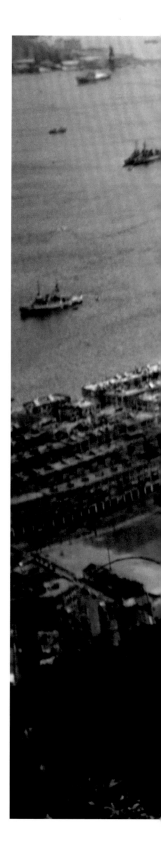

4.6

Looking eastwards from the Peak towards Lei Yue Mun Pass, across the graceful sweep of the 1920s Wanchai reclamation to Causeway Bay, the demolished Morrison Hill and Happy Valley. This photograph was taken in the 1950s.

4.7

The Peak Tower above the Peak Tram station commands a panorama of Hong Kong in the 1950s, encompassing the bustling harbour, Kowloon and the New Territories.

4.8

The Peak Stall

Shops for tourists have always been a prominent feature of the Peak since the war. These shops at the Peak in December 1966 sold postcards, sweets and all manner of locally-manufactured souvenirs.

4.9

Another view of the Central district and Admiralty from a hill above Wanchai in the 1950s.

4.10

A close-up view of the financial centre of Hong Kong from the Peak, with ferries running back and forth to Tsimshatsui in September 1960. The half-completed 23-storey Union House stands out from all the buildings along the old Connaught Road praya, while the older Queen's and Prince's Buildings can still be seen in the far right of this photograph.

4.11

An aerial view of Wanchai and Causeway Bay during the final excavation of Morrison Hill for new development in September 1963. The Kowloon Peninsula and the Kai Tak airport runway can be seen on the other side of the harbour.

4.12

An artist painting on the step of a pavilion at the Peak in 1969, with his work displayed for the tourists to buy.

4.13

Looking up from the Peak Café towards the houses on Mount Austin in 1955.

4.14

A group of western visitors walking uphill to the top of the Peak where The Royal Observatory station was located. It seems the weather was not favourable in November 1964 as the 'black ball' signal has been hung from the mast.

4.15

Wealthy expatriates in Hong Kong lived at the Peak and in the Mid-Levels. Their spacious and well-maintained housing presents a strong contrast with the squalid tenements of Kowloon or the squatter huts occupied by Mainland refugees. This photograph taken in November 1964, shows Deacon Inn, the home of the head of well-known local law firm of Deacons at 29B Lugard Road. Any tourist who saw this lovely villa would not imagine that housing in Hong Kong was such a problem for the government in the 1960s.

4.16

Another comfortable expatriate home on the Peak, Edinburgh Villa, in November 1964. Many houses on the Peak were perched on terraces formed by massive retaining walls of granite, with steep cliffs of stone and thick woodland behind them. Overseas visitors staying with relatives on the Peak were always keen to take such photographs to record where they had stayed.

4.17
Two western ladies taking a cigarette break at the Peak with a view of Aberdeen and Ap Lei Chau behind them in July 1962.

4.18

Aberdeen – the populous and tourist-friendly fishing village on the south side of the Island – is hidden by the shoulder of a hill. The island of Ap Lei Chau is easily recognizable in 1955, but completely undeveloped.

4.19

A view of the southern part of the Island
with British barracks and Maryknoll near
Stanley in the 1950s.

4.20

Nightfall in the 1960s converts Hong Kong into a fairyland of lights to which no artist could do justice. Such scenes lingered in the imagination of visitors long after they had returned home. Victoria Harbour is dark and mysterious but dotted with lights against the glittering city, while ferry lights track their progress across the harbour in this long-exposure photograph. Beyond Kowloon's lights, darkness reigns.

Junks, sampans and a typical fishing village - Aberdeen

Wherever there was open water in Hong Kong, you would once have found junks and sampans in large numbers. During bad weather hundreds of these traditional Chinese vessels would be concentrated in the typhoon shelters. Even today, the waterfronts at Aberdeen, Shau Kei Wan, Yau Ma Tei and Tai Po are veritable maritime museums, and the culture of life on these boats is an important part of Hong Kong's intangible heritage. Junks and sampans have always been family concerns. Children learned at a tender age to take their part in the navigation of the family vessel, and it was not uncommon to see the sail of a sampan handled expertly by a little girl of less than ten years. In Victoria Harbour, junks were used for the transportation of imports and exports, while sampans ferried passengers from merchant ships and sold souvenirs to visitors.

Fishing was a major industry in Hong Kong both before and after the war years, but fishing was not restricted just to fishing boats. Bamboo fishing platforms raised on stilts over the water might be seen almost anywhere around the coast in the 1950s. These platforms were rickety structures held together by bamboo poles tied with a few links of anchor cable. The fishing net could be raised and lowered easily and efficiently, making this a very effective means of catching fish swimming close to the shore. This traditional way of fishing was widely used by both single fishermen and also on a much larger, almost industrial scale in Hong Kong and Macau.

Aberdeen, a large fishing village that has always boasted countless boats, junks and sampans, is believed to have been one of the original settlements on Hong Kong Island before the arrival of the British. To most Chinese, the name 'Aberdeen' is a mystery, for they call it 'Little Hong Kong' or Heung Gong Jai (香港仔). 'Aberdeen' was the name given to the settlement in 1845 by Sir John Davis, the second governor of Hong Kong, naming it after Lord Aberdeen, the British secretary of state for foreign affairs at the time. The original Chinese name of Shek Pai Wan (石排灣) continues to be used by local residents to this day. Interestingly, Aberdeen was one of the first two villages that was renamed instead of using a phonetic translation from the original Chinese name. [1]

1

The other town is Stanley, also named in 1845 by Sir John Davis, after Lord Stanley, the British secretary of state for war and the colonies (1841-45) and later prime minister as Lord Derby (1852, 1858-59, 1866-68). Stanley was the largest village of Hong Kong Island, with the Cantonese name of Chek-chu (赤柱); see Otto C.C. Lam, *Master Insight*, *https://www.master-insight.com*, '從香港首批街道命名，到「赤柱」、「香港仔」如何變成 Stanley 和 Aberdeen', January 2017.

Compared with Shau Kei Wan, the other large fishing village on the north-eastern shore of Hong Kong Island, Aberdeen was more conveniently situated for tourists. Just twenty minutes by car from town, or a little longer on bus route No. 7, Aberdeen has been a major tourist attraction since the 1950s when it featured in the 1955 Hollywood film 'Love is a Many Splendoured Thing', but it was also popular for visits by local residents wanting to have a day out on the southern side of the island. The naturally sheltered cove of Aberdeen was brimming with junks and sampans, and as soon as visitors arrived at the bustling waterfront they were besieged by groups of sampan girls, each one trying to entice a customer to use her sampan: 'Come for a row in my boat, Sir!' For as long as tourists were onboard enjoying the unfamiliar sights of Aberdeen Harbour, these deceptively strong girls would grasp their heavy steering oars and propel their boats around the crowded waterways.

Aberdeen's greatest attraction was its floating restaurants – 'Yu Lee Tai ', 'Tai Pak' and the 'Sea Palace'. Since the 'Yu Lee Tai' disappeared in the 1960s and the 'Jumbo' did not come into existence until the 1970s, most of the photos taken in the 1950s and 1960s show only two of the floating restaurants. Taking a sampan out to one of these floating restaurants was a great adventure for many tourists. Climbing aboard, diners would inspect tanks of live fish to choose their main course. An assortment of exotic seafood – parrot fish, garoupa, white snapper, abalone, top shell, prawns, lobsters and crabs – was always available to be cooked in typical Cantonese style …. a cuisine famed far and wide for its delicate flavours. Visitors left the floating restaurants feeling that they had eaten like kings.

Aberdeen was undoubtedly a MUST visit tourist attraction in Hong Kong during the 1950s and 1960s, so numerous photographs of this part of Hong Kong have survived in private collections around the world.

5.1

Taken at sunset in the typhoon shelter near Yau Ma Tei in Victoria Harbour in November 1967, these boat children are familiar with their watery playground, disregarding all the troubles in life while playing carefree games on their small sampans. Their silhouettes in the sunset form a memorable picture of a lifestyle that has now largely disappeared from Hong Kong's waters.

5.2

A fishing junk with its nets extended in the
harbour, November 1964.

5.3

The period of the 1950s and 1960s was the time of the post-war baby boom, with each family having at least five or six children. A special feature of Hong Kong families was that the eldest sibling would often have to take care of the younger ones while both parents were working. In this photograph taken on 15 May 1966, the eldest sister, who is about 10 years old, is rowing the family boat to the shore while taking care of her younger siblings.

5.4

Fishermen repairing their nets and getting ready for the next off-shore fishing expedition in September 1969.

5.5

November 1967. Hong Kong's young boat people were all physically strong, a good training for standing firm against life's many storms.

5.6

Transporting supplies had always been the main source of income for boat-owners. Taken in June 1962, this photograph of traditional harbour transport showing coal being carried in individual rattan baskets is a scene that has long since disappeared from Hong Kong waters.

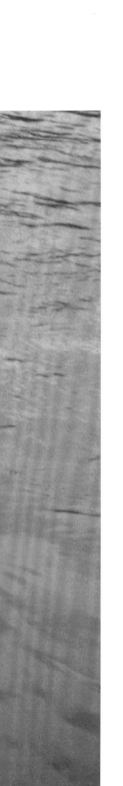

An era without containers
Boxes of goods for import or export loaded onto a fishing boat in Hong Kong waters in November 1964.

5.8

This photograph taken in October 1960
shows a cargo of clay pots that have been
transported by in a Mainland Chinese junk
from Guangzhou to Hong Kong for sale.

5.9

Fishing boats were often used to transport large machines and other goods. This photograph, taken at wintertime during the 1950s, shows coolies who are about to unload big wooden boxes. During the Korean war, an embargo was imposed on China by the United States, so junks from Hong Kong were used to smuggle goods into the Mainland. Fishermen monopolized this illegal trade with the Mainland, earning a great deal of money in the process.

5.10

Junks and sampans gathering around a merchant ship in Victoria Harbour in 1960. Hong Kong boat people supplied goods and services to British merchant and navy ships as early as the First Opium War in the 1840s.

5.11

Fiercely competitive fisherfolk selling souvenirs on Victoria Harbour in the 1950s. These boats peddled souvenirs to the large cruise liners anchored in the harbour. Passengers who had just arrived in Hong Kong were charmed by such activities. Looking down from the deck of their liner, tourists could select and pay for their souvenirs, which would be delivered in a net at the end of a long pole.

5.12

Various villages in Hong Kong had sold dry salted fish as a sideline since early colonial times, an activity that often became the main source of income for fishermen. In the early years, salted fish from Hong Kong was also exported to mainland China, with traders from Guangzhou frequently coming to Hong Kong to purchase fish products. In this photograph taken in December 1963, a child in a fishing village in Tai Po, New Territories, takes responsibility for looking after his family's salted fish as it dries in the sun. The mountain in the distance is Pat Sin Leng.

5.15

Fishing nets supported by bamboo poles were used by these residents of a New Territories village in the 1950s.

5.14

Close to the shore near Cheung Chau, a fisherman sets his net at sunset; he will wait for small fish to swim into the net during the evening. This traditional fishing method used by fishermen in Hong Kong and Macau can now only be seen in photographs such as this, taken in the 1950s.

5.16

A quiet fishing village in the New Territories
in the 1950s.

5.17

A panoramic view of Aberdeen fishing village in September 1960. Many wharves and warehouses can be seen on both sides of Aberdeen Harbour.

5.18

By the 1960s, Aberdeen had become a famous tourist attraction, growing prosperous due to the large number of fishing boats. This photograph taken in May 1969 contrasts the traditional boats on the harbour and the temporary squatter huts on the hillside with the newer multi-storey residential buildings along the shoreline.

5.19

Sampans were the major means of transport in Aberdeen Harbour in the 1950s. Sampan girls played an important role in the economy of the fishing village.

5.20

Sampan girls on the harbourside, ready to
pick up tourists in December 1967.

5.21

A smiling sampan girl waiting for passengers at Aberdeen in the 1950s.

Chapter 5 : Junks, sampans and a typical fishing village - Aberdeen   **227**

5.22

Contestants paddling hard during the dragon boat race at Aberdeen fishing village in 1950s.

5.23

The roof tops of boats are used to dry fish
and seafood in January 1965.

In the fishing districts of Shau Kei Wan, Cheung Chau, Tai Po, Sai Kung, Tai O and Tap Mun, fishermen who did not go out to sea would dock their unseaworthy or damaged boats in typhoon shelters. Boats like these docked by the shore in 1955 would become permanent homes for the fishermen, but living conditions were typically very unsanitary, with all types of filth trapped in the mud around the boats.

5.25

Groups of boat women loitering near
Aberdeen fishing village in the 1950s.

5.26

A well-dressed lady surrounded by boat people at the entrance of the Tai Pak floating restaurant near Aberdeen Village in the 1950s.

5.27

The main street of Aberdeen in the 1960s.
Advertisements could be seen on every
street corner and building.

5.28

The old Aberdeen Main Road was where the fishermen and Hakka farmers gathered. This photograph taken in the 1950s shows the main street of Aberdeen with its three-storey tenement houses. The shops on the ground floor include Shing Cheung Goldsmith at no. 138 Aberdeen Main Road, On Cheung Wine Shop at no. 134, and Lee On Pawn Shop at no. 64.

5.29

Floating restaurants started to appear in Aberdeen as early as 1920, and many more restaurants were established after the War. This early-1950s photograph shows the worn-out floating restaurant 'Sam Yat' laying outside Aberdeen typhoon shelter with the old Tin Hau Temple behind.

5.30
Side view of the two-level Tai Pak Fong
floating restaurant in the 1950s.

5.31

Floating restaurants were popular tourist attractions in Aberdeen Harbour. The 'Tai Pak' floating restaurant was the largest in the 1950s. It started as a simple two-level wooden landing boat with no special decoration until the new 105-foot long 'Tai Pak Fong' was purpose-built in 1952.

5.32

Aberdeen's typhoon shelter has long been a significant tourist attraction which managed to preserve many of the characteristics of a floating village community. In 1958, two large and elaborate floating restaurants Tai Pak and Sea Palace, the later was built as a competitor to the Tai Pak, attracted tourists looking for fresh seafood.

5.33

Choosing live seafood was a 'must' for any tourist eating on one of the Aberdeen floating restaurants. A fisherman holding a large New Zealand lobster boards the restaurant from his small Tai Pak Fong sampan to show this delicacy to tourists in the late 1950s.

5.34

Enjoying a seafood meal like a king in his palace was not beyond the means of most tourists visiting Aberdeen Harbour. A western tourist is caught on film inside a deserted Tai Pak floating restaurant in November 1967.

Chapter 6

Holy Mother Church

The Roman Catholic Cathedral of the Immaculate Conception in the 1950s

The original Catholic Cathedral in Wellington Street was the first church to be erected on Hong Kong Island in 1843. Little is known about this early church, known as St Saviour's Cathedral, until after the fire of 1859 which seriously damaged the building. The newly renovated church, dedicated to the Immaculate Conception of the Blessed Virgin Mary in 1860, was a much larger and more highly decorated structure with five altars and space for around 1,000 worshippers. Over time, the Wellington Street neighbourhood in Central became very crowded and was eventually considered undesirable for religious activities. With a strong demand for a larger church to cater for the needs of a rapidly increasing Catholic population, Bishop Raimondi decided to build a new cathedral between Caine Road and the Glenealy ravine. Construction on the new Cathedral of the Immaculate Conception started in 1883 but it was not opened for worship until 1888. It is a Gothic Revival building designed by the London architectural firm of Crawley and Company. Although damaged by Japanese shelling on 12 December 1941, it remained in use throughout the war. After the war, major renovations were carried out, including the demolition of the bell tower at the west end, the addition of a lantern to the central tower, and increased space for new pews and confessionals. Since then, the Cathedral has undergone major repairs once every two decades.

This series of colour images of the Cathedral was taken in the winter between 1954 and 1955, after the coronation of the statue of the Virgin Mary, an event which attracted over 30,000 people. Many structural changes have taken place since these photographs were taken. The original pipe organ, installed in the choir loft in 1921, was still functioning in the 1950s. The original grotto of Our Lady of Lourdes was already located near the Sacristy door at the east end. The elaborate high altar at the east end beyond the central tower featured a timber-carved statue of Our Lady, presented by Catholic students, and a large wooden crucifix. The original baptismal font with its steeple-like cover was set on a platform near the main entrance, next to the spiral iron staircase to the organ loft.

Major changes to the exterior of the cathedral and its grounds have taken place since the 1950s. A handsome porch on the Glenealy side was demolished to make way for the Diocesan Centre in 1965. The pleasant gardens that surrounded the cathedral have been entirely removed and concreted over for car-parking. The bas-reliefs of saints in three roundels in the tracery over the main entrance are now gone. Indeed, the magnificently commanding location of the cathedral has been masked by the modern buildings that now surround it. One of these 1950s photographs shows how the cathedral towered over the surrounding urban landscape, almost as if it had been erected on top of a cliff. There is no doubt that the Cathedral of the Immaculate Conception remains an architectural masterpiece to this day, even though its beautiful outlook has been blocked by modern skyscrapers. These colour images of the Cathedral bear witness to the evolving development of the Catholic community in Hong Kong during the 1950s.

6.1

A magnificent view from Caine Road towards the Peak in the 1950s, showing the various Catholic buildings erected on Robinson Road above the mansions that had once been used as residences by C.B. Hillier, Assistant Magistrate of Police, and Robert Dundas Cay, Colonial Registrar, in the 1840s.

6.2

The Catholic Cathedral of the Immaculate Conception at 16 Caine Road, Mid-Levels was opened for worship in 1888. The construction cost was US$15,400. In the early days, photographs of the Cathedral were all in black-and-white. This photograph taken from the Zoological and Botanical Gardens in the 1950s shows the entire Cathedral and its garden surroundings, with Victoria Harbour in the background.

6.3

This close-up of the majestic cathedral in the 1950s accentuates its Gothic Revival architectural style. The roof, which was partly destroyed by Japanese action during the war, was later repaired and a lantern added to the central tower in the major renovation of 1952.

6.4

A view of the Cathedral from Glenealy in
the 1950s.

6.5

The main entrance of the Cathedral from
the Gleanealy pathway running up from
Caine Road.

6.6

A magnificent view of Victoria Harbour from the Cathedral in the 1950s. The massive platform-terrace on which the Cathedral stands can be clearly seen in this image.

6.7

The Tower in front of the Cathedral was demolished to make way for the construction of a school in 1947, but this photograph shows the old arched staircase next to the Cathedral that led up to Catholic buildings on Robinson Road.

6.8

The porch facing Glenealy with its angel above the arch. This porch was demolished to make way for the building of the Diocesan Centre in 1965.

6.9

A colourful statue of Our Lady of Lourdes in the grotto outside the Cathedral in the 1950s.

6.10

A stone and metal crucifix next to the
Lourdes grotto.

6.11

The cathedral's pipe organ in the choir loft was still functioning when this photograph was taken in the 1950s.

The original baptismal font next to the spiral stairway to the organ loft in the aisle next to the main entrance, 1950s.

6.13

The high altar situated in the apse of the cathedral beyond the central tower. An elaborate arched baldacchino on top of the altar housed a timber-carved statue of Our Lady, presented by Catholic students, while a large wooden crucifix stood above the tabernacle. The high altar, where Mass was celebrated, was the focal point of the whole Cathedral until the altar was moved to a new raised platform under the central crossing following the liturgical reforms of the Second Vatican Council in the 1960s.

Chapter 7

People and Life

There was a peculiar charm about Hong Kong for most tourists, especially for those who were avid amateur photographers. Hong Kong's streets, for anyone arriving fresh to the East, were an amazing pageant, ever changing, ever new. After admiring the city's architectural beauties, the tourist was mostly interested in the vibrant street life, especially in the Chinese quarters of the city. There was always something novel, something quaint for the observant visitor, be it straining coolies, the city's human beasts of burden, hauling anything from cargo to heavy trucks; or a hawker's mysterious wares, ranging from live poultry from the New Territories to quaint teapots from Guangdong, laid out in some narrow alley. Everywhere people were selling goods, in shops, in stalls, in crowded markets, and in peddlers' packs – articles which the newcomer sometimes recognized with a peculiar sense of incongruity, others which were mysterious beyond words.

For scenes of Chinese daily life, the Central Market area and the eastern and western portions of Queen's Road were favoured choices. Here splendid photographs could be obtained of Chinese hucksters, rickshaw pullers, bottle sellers, metal workers, furniture carvers, barbers and letter-writers. It was here that food stalls lured the hungry with inviting aromas. Not far away, Chinese eating houses with their long signboards or tall decorative plaques traced with intricate designs or splashed with arresting Chinese characters hung over the doorways. Here, half-naked kitchen-boys worked in smoky kitchens, while succulent smells hung heavily over the chattering crowds of diners.

At the western end of the Praya, between Kennedy Town and Wing Lok Street, good photographs could be taken of coolies loading and discharging junks. In the side streets leading off Queen's Road, it was a common sight to come across one or more coolies carrying heavy loads suspended from their bamboo poles, a method of haulage that had been used for hundreds of years in South China. The wharves were particularly good for finding interesting photographic subjects. Every day, steamers arrived from Canton and Macau, bringing thousands of strangers to Hong Kong, who were often stopped by policemen for identity checks as they exited the wharves.

In Tsimshatsui, a turbaned Indian guard standing watch outside a dance hall might oblige the polite tourist by posing for a photograph. All these subjects offered good opportunities for life photography, and many tourists had no hesitation or scruples in making the most of these opportunities.

No visitor would miss photographing the children of Hong Kong. The number of children in Hong Kong was astounding during this period. Out of a population of just over three million in the mid-1960s, there were 510,000 children under the age of five and a total of more than one million children of all ages. With around one third of the population consisting of children, it is not surprising that they were such popular photographic subjects. Down any quiet street, a little girl might be seen sitting on a bench doing her homework; or another who had fallen asleep over the newspapers she was selling. Some of the children had to eat on the streets, while others carried younger siblings on their backs in the squatter areas. Hong Kong children knew how to look after each other from an early age. Those children who did not go to school fended for themselves, roaming the streets and hoping to be able to beg a few cents or pick up some discarded food in one of the tourist areas.

Tourists might also happen upon colourful local customs, the likes of which they had never observed before. In the 1950s, the funeral of a wealthy Chinese resident was an impressive spectacle. The procession – sometimes more than a mile in length – was headed by a band of musicians, dressed in uniforms. The cortege included a variety of gorgeous symbolic ornaments carried by perspiring coolies; while professional mourners attired in white drooped limply in the arms of their supporters. The coffin, sometimes weighing nearly half a ton, was borne on a decorated litter.

Fireworks played an essential part at most Chinese functions. The Lunar New Year was heralded by a deafening fusillade of crackers, and the Dragon Boat Festival presented another opportunity for glorious bursts of noise. Dragon boats were slim and unstable craft, expertly propelled by forty or fifty paddlers, with the timing of the strokes controlled by two men beating a drum amidships. Races were run annually in Victoria Harbour, Aberdeen and other large fishing villages such as Tai Po.

Visitors found that many aspects of life in Hong Kong were hidden, and few tourists had time to discover all of the richness of local life in the 1950s and 1960s, but those who did manage to seek out the Chinese way of life in Hong Kong realized that it was totally distinctive and very memorable.

7.1

Rickshaw No. 414

Rickshaws servicing Hong Kong Island were very different from those in Kowloon. While the Kowloon rickshaws provided services mainly for tourists in the Tsimshatsui area, those on the Island helped residents transport items of various sizes over short distances. This photograph shows a rickshaw puller in September 1960 waiting outside a busy shop on Queen's Road Central to transport goods for customers. In the 1950s, the official fare was flat rate of 20 cents irrespective of distance as long as the hire did not exceed ten minutes, and 30 cents for every additional period of 10 minutes or 60 cents for every additional half hour. The fare had increased to 50 cents for every five minutes by the 1960s.

7.2

The historic Central Market was located at the junction of Queen's Road Central and Jubilee Street, where pedestrians and cars would fight for space on the roadway. This photograph, taken in September 1960, captures a swarm of pedestrians, including a woman in a cool floral dress, about to cross Jubilee Street.

7.3

The entrance to the market near 122 Queen's Road Central and Graham Street in September 1960 indicates the narrowness of the street, always busy with women doing their grocery shopping with their children.

7.4

Another view of Graham Street showing the sign board for the Chiu Tai Local Bank.

The small shops on both sides of Pottinger Street, Central, sold different products during different times. The small shops on the stone slabs still exist sixty years after these photographs were taken. The only differences are the dress and demeanour of the pedestrians. In September 1960, passers-by put on wooden clogs and plastic flip-flops, which were popular at that time. They enjoyed moments of peace in this busy area; having bought a nail-clipper in a small shop nearby, this coolie is trimming his toenails on the side of the street.

7.6

Stone Slab Street was divided into two sections with one being narrower, near to where the Yung Kee Restaurant was originally located at 30A Pottinger Street. At the top of this photograph taken in September 1960, the Yung Kee signboard is hidden among the shops. Apart from serving the usual dishes in Cantonese cuisine – congee, noodles, and rice dishes – and providing takeaway services, the most famous Yung Kee dish was their signature crispy roasted goose.

A shopkeeper in a cooked meat stall is here seen wrapping pieces of chopped roast pork for a client in Central in September 1961.

7.8

A shop attendant selecting soy chicken according to his customer's preference in September 1961.

7.9

Two coolies using a pole to carry a heavy barrel, full of oil, to a market place shop in the 1960s.

7.10

Two coolies delivering a live pig in a rattan basket, again using a bamboo pole, running steadily through the market place in Central in the 1950s.

Hong Kong's Chinese population was concentrated in the narrow streets, and many of those who sold livestock set up roadside stalls. Farmers from the New Territories shown in this photograph from October 1960 carried live poultry in traditional baskets suspended from a shoulder pole, to sell on busy streets in the urban area of Kowloon. Due to outbreaks of avian influenza in the early twenty-first century, these scenes of live poultry being sold on the streets are forever gone.

Live poultry was bought because of its freshness. In order to check the health of a chicken, the housewife would look at their hindquarters and blow the tail feathers to check the overall condition of the bird. This method of examining poultry, now regarded as a highly risky undertaking, is shown in this photograph taken in November 1964.

7.13

Shan Hoi Restaurant, Long Shan and Ming Shing Barber Shop, at 2 Aberdeen Street, provided residents with everyday services. This photograph, taken in September 1960, captures the wet and slippery surface of the steeply-inclined Aberdeen Street after rain. Pedestrians needed to pay extra attention when walking on these streets.

7.14

Women gathering around a stall on the roadside during the hot summer in Aberdeen on 8 August 1967.

7.15

Lunchtime was the busiest time for markets in Central. Office boys or messengers of large corporations, despite being busy, would often sneak to the old Central Market to buy food from roadside stalls. In this photograph from September 1960, a messenger has purchased a pear from a roadside stall to quench his thirst. The hawkers selling pears had excellent knife skills, peeling a pear in just a few seconds for immediate consumption.

7.16

A woman preparing her stall for another day of selling vegetables in a side street in Central, September 1960.

7.17

The area close to the harbourfront on Des Voeux Road West in Sheung Wan was the hub of dried seafood shops. This 1969 photograph features the Mao Lee Dried Seafood Shop at 144 Des Voeux Road West. Trucks were invariably parked outside these shops, waiting to load or unload goods.

7.18

Many Hong Kong housewives liked to visit sweet stores. In this photograph taken in the 1950s, branded goods were put in prominent places inside the store, including Eagle condensed milk from Nestle and Longevity condensed milk imported from the Netherlands. The stall hawker is holding his scales up to show that the weight is accurate.

7.19

Taken outside 118A Hollywood Road in March 1964, this photograph shows a coolie carrying restaurant chairs on a shoulder pole. The delivery car of Hai Chan Banquet Catering Expert is parked in the background. It was a popular trend in the 1960s for big families and companies to use the banquet catering services, especially on festive occasions.

7.20

Under the blazing sun in June 1962, a bronze-skinned worker shoulders heavy steel cables as he swiftly crosses the road. In the background is King Fook Jewellery at 5 Bonham Strand and Wing Hang Bank at 163-167 Queen's Road Central.

7.21

Working as a coolie, the lowest form of unskilled labour, was the commonest form of work found by many grass-roots people in Hong Kong. Regardless of gender, as long as it would enable the worker to earn a living, it would do. The man and woman in this photograph taken in the 1950s were moving large canvas sacks from the dockside using a shoulder pole. That women were forced to do such heavy manual labour appalled many westerner visitors to Hong Kong.

For the fashion-conscious woman in Hong Kong, there were department stores that sold imported goods as well as many local fashion manufacturers who tailor-made clothes for the discerning. In this photograph taken in July 1955, the lady in a white cheongsam is passing a fashion boutique in Causeway Bay in a hurry, but cannot help being attracted by the new designs displayed in the shop window. The reflection in the shop window shows the signboard of Dairy Farm at Windsor House on the opposite side of the street.

7.23

An elegantly dressed Chinese woman in a silk printed cheongsam standing on the harbourfront in the 1950s.

7.24

An old lady standing in a carpark near Kowloon Tong in the 1960s.

7.25

A rickshaw puller running past a motor car outside Shui Hing Department store on Cameron Road in Tsimshatsui on 28 October 1964.

7.26

Heung Wan Hoi

The old barracks on Canton Road, Tsimshatsui, near Austin Road had not been used for a long time, but many soldiers and tourists would still visit the area. In August 1958, a turbaned Indian guard is patrolling the street outside the Heung Wan Hoi dancehall.

7.27

Fruits on sale at Tai Po Market in the
winter of 1956.

7.28

A busy market place located between Shun Yee Street and Kimberley Street in Tsimshatsui in July 1962. Lily's Garden Café & Restaurant was situated at Nos. 9-11 Kimberley Street, with its back-door entrance shown in this photograph.

7.29

A street hawker on Berwick Street, Shek Kip Mei, in October 1960. The mother is seen multi-tasking – holding her naked child while at the same time peeling a pear for her customer. Trays of soft drink bottles behind her are ready for recycling and re-use by A.S. Watsons, Tropi orange juice and Bireley's.

7.30

Street hawkers at the junction of Pei Ho Street and Berwick Street, Shek Kip Mei, busily selling fruit and snacks near the Palace Theatre in October 1960. Street hawkers had used bamboo poles to carry their rattan baskets since early colonial times. The rattan baskets had not changed over the century, but the hawkers' clothes were now far less traditional.

7.31

Movie-going was a popular form of entertainment for the residents of resettlement estates in the 1960s. The Palace Theatre, located at the junction of Pei Ho Street and Berwick Street, was the local entertainment venue for residents of that district. The theatre commenced business in 1953 and was air-conditioned, a great luxury for people living in the estates. In October 1960, 'An Uncle's Sacrifice' was showing.

'An Uncle's Sacrifice'

In September 1960, the Palace Theatre in Shek Kip Mei was showing the first-run Cantonese film 'An Uncle's Sacrifice'. Fung Fung was the director and the scriptwriter, while his daughter, Petrina Fung Bo-bo, played the lead role of Mak Shiu-kuen. This was Petrina Ho's sixth movie. At that time, large and colourful printed advertisements were not yet common, with almost all cinema advertisements being hand-painted. These were the early days of the advertising industry in Hong Kong.

7.33

In the 1950s and 1960s, the Hong Kong film industry was rapidly developing, with cinematic output topping the world. These eye-catching advertisements in October 1960 are the type of large and colourful hand-painted billboards that could be seen in many heavily populated areas.

7.34

Tourists watching Cantonese Opera in the 1950s at a local theatre where fruit is being served to the audience. Lam Ka Sing, a famous young actor, is on the stage performing as an ancient Chinese army general.

7.35

Shanghainese food

After 1949, a large number of Shanghainese refugees came to Hong Kong. In both Tsimshatsui and Causeway Bay, numerous restaurants were opened by Shanghainese. Shanghainese restauranteurs adapted the cuisine to suit the climatic conditions of South China, so drinking Coke while eating Youtiao, dumplings and scallion cakes became very popular. The jolly owner of a Shanghainese restaurant is photographed in June 1962 by a passing tourist.

7.36

The Dai Pai Dong (outdoor food stall) was a central component of the local Hong Kong culinary culture that could be seen everywhere in 1960s, providing both Chinese and Western food for residents. This Dai Pai Dong is serving congee and noodles in a squatter area in September 1960.

7.37

A lavishly decorated wedding chair being carried by four coolies along Chatham Road in Tsimshatsui during the 1950s.

Life and death are paths one must travel. A funeral procession gathers outside the International Funeral Parlour at 41 Lockhart Road, Wan Chai, in the 1950s. The funeral parlour, which was famous at that time, was managed by Leung Chi-fung.

7.39

'The Sky is Red'

An elaborate funeral display in a Wan Chai street in the 1950s outside a cinema showing the Western film 'The Sky is Red'. These colourful funeral displays and the erotic movie advertisements form an interesting contrast.

7.40

In February 1966, Fuk Shing Ho shop in Tai Po market is being treated to a lion dance. The leader of the dance team would put the red packet received from the shop-owner in a pocket of his traditionally styled long-sleeved jacket, made in typical Shunde 'heong-wan-sa' fabric.

7.41

Every Chinese New Year, martial arts associations would form teams to perform lion dances in the villages of the New Territories. This photograph, taken during the Chinese New Year in 1967, features one such lion dance team which has seized this annual money-making opportunity.

Old Hong Kong in colour

The Cheung Chau Da Jiu ceremony and processions captured in these photographs on 9 May 1962 were annual celebrations that attracted many visitors to Cheung Chau. Large festive display boards welcoming the Governor were placed along main roads and the waterfront. Dragon dances were an indispensable part of the festivities. The meaning and origin of Cheung Chau Bun Festival is lost in the mists of time, but one version suggests that the pirate Cheung Po Tsai killed many local merchants on Tung Wan Beach when they failed to pay a ransom he had demanded. Another version claims that a typhoon damaged several fishing boats in Cheung Chau and killed many fishermen. Residents therefore initiated a vegetarian 'da jiu' ritual so that the spirits of the deceased could rest in peace. While it used to be a tradition for those taking part in the Cheung Chau Bun Festival to fast for three days, this practice has long disappeared.

Dragon dancers run through the floral plaque with welcome words for the visit of the Governor of Hong Kong.

7.44

On 9 May 1962, members of local martial arts associations hold banners during the Bun Festival parade, passing by the Cheung Chau Chinese Chamber of Commerce and the Fish Marketing Organization. The top right corner of the photo shows a hand-painted lantern used during Cheung Chau Bun Festival provided by the Far East Bank. The Far East Bank was founded by the late Mr Deacon Chiu and mainly served the New Territories and outlying islands. A group of tourists can be seen in the lower right corner.

7.45

A young Western man having his photograph taken at the Repulse Bay Hotel on 19 June 1954, with Repulse Bay beach in the background.

7.46

Water activities were always popular among expatriates living in Hong Kong. This woman in a fashionable swimming suit drives a speed boat near Shek O in the 1950s. .

7.47

Ling Kwong Primary School children on their way home from school are stopped by a visitor for a photograph at 40 Shing Tak Street in Ma Tau Wan, Kowloon, in October 1964.

7.48

A group of girls gathered in the sitting room of a large house on Hong Kong Island after school in the 1950s, practising for a drama performance under the direction of their teacher.

7.49

On a sunny day in 1955, four young boys in the company of an older guide, visit a the brightly coloured exhibit extolling the message that 'agricultural families are charitable and willing to give', a scene designed by the See Wah Art Society. Three of the boys appear to be more interested in the foreigner taking the photograph.

7.50

Children living in the urban areas faced an overcrowded living environment. They would use whatever materials they could find to have some fun. These children are drawing on the footpath with chalk in February 1957.

7.51

A well-dressed boy from a wealthy family standing in front of a camera and watch store in Tsimshatsui in December 1966. From his facial expression, he was not interested in these adult toys, and did not want to go into the store. He is happy to lean against the shop, quietly waiting for his parents to come out.

7.52

The Central and Western District was traditionally known for its many famous schools. In busy Aberdeen Street at 3 p.m. in September 1960, children finishing school are passing by the Hu Lap Fung Medical Clinic and Tsang On Tong. Parents often brought their children home from school. Many other children without school uniforms are playing on the streets.

7.53

At a street-side barber shop in the early 1960s, children are sitting on a wooden bench and reading comics while waiting for their haircut, disregarding the barber busily cutting hair. Reading was a privilege sixty years ago; children nowadays bury their heads in mobile phones rather than comics.

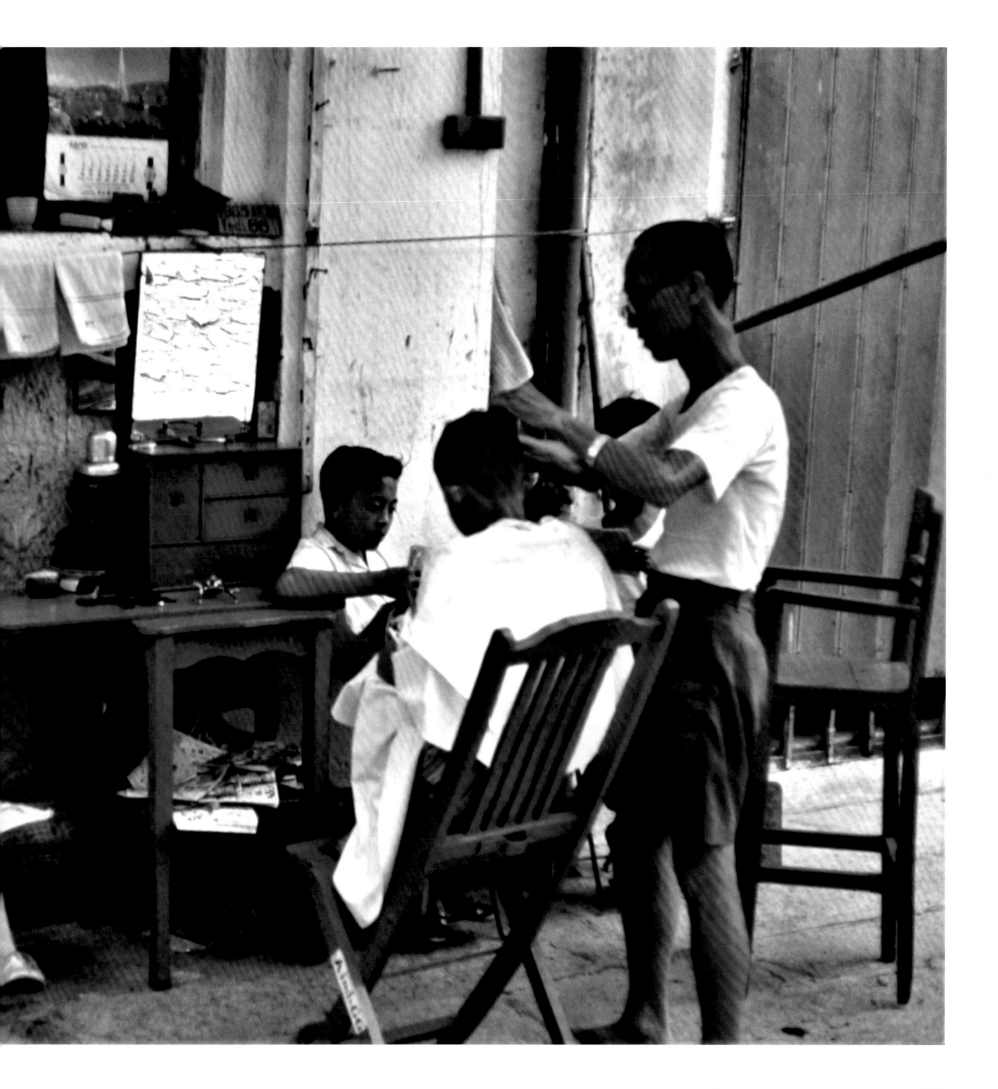

In the squatter area on the hillside at Shau Kei Wan in October 1960, residents are queuing for water during a period of water-rationing. It was the women, with their children, who carried water buckets of different shapes and sizes to government standpipes. Together, they waited for the water supply to commence at designated times and then carried back to their huts the amount of drinking water needed by the family for the whole day. Children born after the war went through hard times with their parents in the 1950s and 1960s. As they grew up, they usually worked hard and without complaint, forming the foundations of the 'Hong Kong spirit'.

Children idling in their fishing village are astonished when a tourist takes their picture on 10 July 1965.

7.56

The widespread poverty in Hong Kong during the 1950s was reflected in the children without proper clothing on the streets. In November 1959, a group of visitors has stopped at a fishing village and are being asked for change by a group of shoe-less children.

7.57

Village life within the walled village of Kam Tin in the 1960s.

Chapter 8

Resettlement

Hong Kong has a land area of less than 400 square miles – little more than half the size of Greater London and not much more than the city of New York – yet by the end of 1969, more than four million people were crowded into this tiny place. After experiencing several post-war population booms, the population was increasing at a rate of 100,000 a year. Hong Kong therefore became the most densely populated place on earth in the 1960s. Finding shelter had always been a problem for people wanting to settle down in Hong Kong. Many new immigrants in the 1950s and 1960s found that they could only find shelter in the vacant spaces within the urban areas. Houses were illegally constructed on hillsides and other marginal plots of land without government authorization. Those who had greater resources at their disposal would construct their houses from stone and brick, while the less privileged could only afford scraps of wood and tin plate.

In the 1950s, wooden huts constituted the most convenient and affordable form of housing for newcomers from the Mainland, with squatters occupying many of the hillsides around Kowloon and on Hong Kong Island. The disastrous Shek Kip Mei fire of 1953 burned out hundreds of ramshackle squatter huts and rendered thousands homeless. In response to this crisis, the government started building resettlement estates which would eventually fill up large expanses of vacant and reclaimed land. By the end of 1969, there were more than 480 blocks of resettlement buildings in four different designs housing 1,060,008 persons. The phase-one Mark I seven-storey block was the first of its kind built across Kowloon and Hong Kong Island. Rooms in these buildings rented for only $10 to $18 per month according to their size and the number of people accommodated, with an average size of 300 square feet per unit and housing five persons. Shek Kip Mei became the first 'Low Cost Housing Estate' in Hong Kong. The ground floor of each block usually contained shops, and each floor above had long corridors running the entire length of each side of the distinctive 'H' shape. There were no special areas for drying clothes, with washed clothing being stuck out on poles along balconies, giving passers-by the impression that these blocks were decorated with flags. Internal passage-ways were quickly cluttered with all sorts of odds and ends. Residents had to share public toilets, bathrooms and laundry areas. These places became a vital link between all residents, where they established new social contacts outside their small and compressed living quarters. There were playgrounds for children, and marketplaces with shops selling all types of products, where stall-holders competed with hawkers peddling their wares to the impoverished residents. There were kindergartens and primary schools set up by charity or missionary groups on the rooftops on each block. These resettlement estates were like miniature cities, each reflecting on a small scale the wide diversity of post-war Hong Kong.

Other organizations provided inexpensive housing for white-collar and higher income workers. The Java Street housing scheme completed in 1957 was one of the first to be developed by the Hong Kong Government. It housed 1,995 families totaling 16,000 people. In this estate, the rent was not particularly inexpensive, with average rents ranging from $76 to $170 per month for a 4-to-8 person flat, roughly one third of the monthly income of a working-class family. The size of the flat allocated depended on the number of members in the family applying, and allocation of flats was made from long waiting lists. Another new housing estate at Choi Hung that accommodated 96,000 people from the middle-income group was situated in Kowloon not far from Kai Tak Airport. In these housing estates, the areas between buildings provided plenty of playing space for children. The individual kitchens and bathrooms, although very small, were selling points for people who a higher level of privacy. Small verandahs outside each unit provided a place to dry washed clothes. Facilities inside these housing estates included kindergartens, proper schools, banks and shopping centres, which all helped to create a strong sense of community.

Resettlement estates were a by-product of the population pressure exerted on Hong Kong in the post-war years, and for those who moved into them from shabby squatter homes, they created closely-knit neighborhoods with a sense of continuity similar to their old lifestyle on the hillsides of Kowloon and Hong Kong Island, but more comfortable and permanent.

8.1

Squatter huts near Sai Wan Ho and Shau Kei Wan in October 1960. The government set up standpipes along this drainage channel to supply drinking water. Residents, including both the young and the elderly, queued each day for fresh water. There was often physical conflict over water supplies in such rudimentary conditions, and it was not unknown for people to be injured in such disputes. This photograph also shows several advertisements for bone-setting clinics: Liu Chi-keung and Wong Yiu-nam from Mong Kok, Yiu Shing from Wan Chai, and Au Tai-ming from Shau Kei Wan.

8.2

Squatter huts built on the hillsides were usually made of timber, due to lower transportation and construction costs. Land was often occupied by people who built new squatter huts, which would then be leased to newly arrived immigrants. This photograph taken in September 1960 shows wooden squatter huts on the slopes behind Shau Kei Wan. Although located in the 'mid-levels', these were very different houses from the gleaming apartments of the Mid-Levels of Hong Kong and Wanchai. There was no town planning and the distribution of huts on the hillside was complicated and messy. Residents had to hike along the hillsides each day when travelling to work in the mornings and returning home in the evenings.

8.3

This two-storey stone bungalow was located in Shau Kei Wan. The ground floor was leased as a shop, while three families lived upstairs. This photograph was taken at noon in September 1960, a perfect time to dry clothes in the scorching sun. Families would hang washing on balconies and in any empty space. Adults and children are staying indoors to avoid getting sunburnt.

The same stone bungalow, shown later on the same day at around 6 pm, just before sunset. Residents have brought in their washing and are busy tidying outside their homes. Workers returning home are passing by.

8.5

The squatter houses on Hong Kong Island and in Kowloon, whether constructed from timber, stone or brick, were generally called 'bungalows'. In 1969, there were fifteen bungalow areas in Hong Kong, with around 58,000 residents waiting for resettlement. The bungalow areas had cafeterias serving food and drinks, such as this one in Sai Wan Ho in October 1960. Hoi Kee Poultry restaurant was at 29 Shing On Street. It was a large cafeteria that served the whole bungalow area, with plum chicken and marinated goose being its specialty dishes. The balcony on the second floor is full of clothes drying, perhaps demonstrating that several families lived there. Wong Yiu Nam's advertisement on the right indicates that his Chinese medicine factory 'Pu Chit Wan' was located in a stone house near Nam On Street, Shau Kei Wan.

8.6

The hills above Sai Wan Ho in October 1960. Terrace farming is still taking place on the hillside, and quite a few stone bungalows beneath the hills were local wineries, including Hap Yik Long, Tai Tak Winery and Tai Yuen Medical Liquor.

8.7

The construction industry in Hong Kong developed rapidly during the 1950s and 1960s. Numerous tenement houses were demolished for reconstruction, creating many jobs in the industry. Here, skilled masonry workers are building a retaining wall next to a hillside sometime in the 1950s.

8.8

The Hong Kong government constructed resettlement buildings on a large scale in the 1950s and 1960s to solve the housing problem faced by large numbers of immigrants and local residents. The first phase of the resettlement scheme was located at Shek Kip Mei. This photograph from October 1960 shows the Shek Kip Mei resettlement estate, referred to in Chinese as 'blocks of seven levels', six years after construction.

8.9

The Shek Kip Mei resettlement area was located next to Berwick Street, Sham Shui Po. In October 1960, the modern resettlement blocks and the Shek Kip Mei Health Centre provide a stark contrast with the wooden squatter houses on the slope in the distance. On the right were older buildings in Sham Shui Po, the new blending rather uncomfortably with the old.

8.10

The first batch of resettlement buildings was constructed after a hill fire broke out near the squatter area of Shek Kip Mei on Christmas day in 1953. The 'new district' was built on the original site, with 29 blocks of Mark I and Mark II buildings to house 64,553 residents. Taken in October 1960, this photograph shows the resettlement buildings between Nam Cheong Street and Woh Chai Street. There was a Police Post on the ground floor of one of the resettlement blocks. The red truck parked on the street is a delivery vehicle belonging to the Tong On Company at 117 Nam Cheong Street.

8.11

The junction of Woh Chai Street and Nam Cheong Street inside the Shek Kip Mei resettlement estate in October 1960. The office of the Shek Kip Mei estate is shown on the ground floor, commonly called 'the office of District Officer' by residents. Residents paid their rent at this office every month. The 'District Officer' was responsible for managing all matters relating to the housing estate and was often involved in conflicts with residents. The job required great diplomatic skills, for it was difficult to please everyone.

8.12

The resettlement estates had to satisfy the many needs of local residents, especially in the area of food supply. The newly opened Leung Lee Meat and Seafood Supply Company shown in this photograph used a traditional five-storey-high advertising display that could be seen from a distance.

8.13

In October 1960, the Chi Shing Meat
Supply Company had recently opened
on the ground floor of Block V, Shek Kip
Mei resettlement estate. Its elaborate
display board thanks customers for their
patronage. The Cheng Shun Kee Store
next door was conveniently located for
grocery shopping.

8.14

Hung Kee Shop, Tak Cheung Wine Shop and Hap Hing Store on the ground floor of a Shek Kip Mei resettlement building in October 1960. Trays of soft drinks were the main sale item in these shops during the summertime.

8.15

Shops on the ground floor of resettlement
buildings included butchers' shops,
wine shops and grocery shops. This
photograph taken in October 1960 shows
idle shopkeepers chatting and reading
newspapers.

8.16

There were both residential units and shops on the ground floor of resettlement estates. Some residents made use of their flats for handicraft jobs to help their families financially. This photograph, taken outside a unit in the Shek Kip Mei resettlement estate in October 1960, shows a mother working on copper tubing with the help of an older son, while younger siblings are playing nearby. This was always a convenient arrangement for taking care of children close to the workspace. In the 1960s, Hong Kong was not a prosperous city for most residents, but no matter how difficult life was, adults would always try to take care of their children, forming very close ties between members of the family. Nowadays, both parents often go out to work and children are left at home to play alone, often developing a lonely and indifferent personality.

The empty spaces between resettlement blocks were often occupied by temporary fruit stalls. This large fruit stall in the Shek Kip Mei resettlement estate in October 1960 has women stall-keepers. A young girl has just returned to her mother from school.

8.18

Mobile barbers on bicycles provided cheap hair-cutting services for residents in resettlement estates. This photograph was taken on the ground floor of block W in the Shek Kip Mei resettlement estate in September 1960. The mother is arranging for the elder brother to have his hair cut, while the younger brother is eating an icicle in his mother's arms. The elder brother is drooling while waiting for his haircut. The poster on the wall invites the registration of new students for a primary school on the rooftop of the resettlement block. The school tuition fee was HK$4 per month.

8.19
Helping each other

An obvious feature of resettlement estates was that every flat housed children. As most adults had to work, those who stayed home, especially the elderly men and women, would take care of each other and help to look after neighbours' children. In September 1963, as some parents go off work, others buy groceries and bring their children home. Elderly neighbours shown here at a typical resettlement block would often be asked to look after children.

8.20

A photogenic mother with her young children is standing outside Block 'L' of the Shek Kip Mei resettlement estate in October 1964.

8.21

The Church World Service

There were various church organizations providing charitable services in Hong Kong's resettlement areas in the 1960s. In September 1963, the van of the Church World Service, an American organization, is parked outside its noodle factory in Kowloon. An expatriate official is discussing arrangements with a local member of staff.

The Church World Society had a branch office and noodle factory in Kowloon in the 1960s, specializing in providing food relief to needy residents. In September 1963, aid workers are preparing to distribute bags of bulgur wheat weighing 100 pounds each to residents in the Shek Kip Mei resettlement estate. Children in the background are waiting excitedly for the distribution.

Most of the people housed in resettlement estates in the 1950s and 1960s had low incomes and lived difficult lives. In this photograph taken in September 1963, an American charity is preparing to distribute relief supplies to residents at Shek Kip Mei. To the residents of communities such as this, these European and American aid workers were welcome guests among those whose lives were so hard. A large number of residents of all ages have gathered to meet the aid workers.

Chapter 9

Macau

Macau was variously described in the early twentieth century as the 'Gem of the Orient Earth' and 'a sleepy, tranquil Latin village with a Chinese as well as a Mediterranean flavour'. It was not yet known as the Monte Carlo or Las Vegas of the East in the 1950s. Macau is located west of Hong Kong, forty-five miles across the Pearl River estuary, a journey of less than an hour today by jetfoil. As Hong Kong's closest neighbour, tourist promotion for Macau has been linked to Hong Kong since the end of the nineteenth century, with tour packages for Macau treated as part of the 'Hong Kong experience'. Unlike the hectic scramble that tourists experienced in the British colony, however, Macau's slow pace and tranquility seemed to be a remarkable survival from a previous age.

To the holiday maker in search of novelty and amusement, Macau provided a congenial field for exploration. Founded by the Portuguese in the sixteenth century, Macau was the earliest European settlement on the South China coast. The city had the ability to transport the visitor's mind to Southern Europe, for it had the feel of the quiet summer seaside hideaways of the Mediterranean, with their quaintly situated fishing ports and clusters of ancient churches. A walk through the narrow streets of the old town was usually accompanied by healthy sea breezes, a welcome escape from the enervating summer heat of Hong Kong. The colonnades and arches of the gracious nineteenth-century houses painted in their pastel pinks, blues, limes and yellows created a sensation of stepping back in time: Macau was a Portuguese city of olden times transplanted into Chinese surroundings, where the key characteristics of European and Chinese lifestyles were deftly and delightfully interwoven. A blending of Mediterranean and Chinese architecture could be found in every quarter of the town, forming an amazingly harmonious style: oriental balconies, western shutters and windows, columns and colonnades, tiled roofs and walls painted in a subtle combination of pastel shades. The worn stone pavements, crumbling and dilapidated, the city walls choked with weeds, and stone monuments covered with creepers, all spoke of times that were past. Around Macau were clustered a host of historic buildings: monasteries, convents, churches, fortresses, battlements, barracks and the Guia Lighthouse.

There is a peculiar charm about Macau that is exceedingly difficult to explain, and to the artist or photographer with eyes open to its beauty, the city has always had a special appeal. The feeling of having walked back in time along the quaint and irregular streets, with their massively built houses and the various trades still being carried on as they were in former centuries, gave Macau a special appeal to people, not just to day-trippers from Hong Kong, but to the many overseas visitors from around the world. Coming as they did from the rush and bustle of modern life, they thoroughly appreciated the restfulness and the leisureliness of Portugal's first settlement on the South China coast.

9.1

A western visitor has just landed and is waiting to be collected at the Macau Hydrofoil terminus in May 1969.

9.2

On the yellowish waters of Macau's Inner
Harbour, the Bishop's Palace can be seen
atop Penha Hill, from where a sweeping
view of the whole city could be seen.
This 1950s photograph shows the lack of
development in this part of Macau, with
the old Moorish Barracks tucked behind
harbourside warehouses along the junk-
choked Inner Harbour.

9.3

In the 1950s, fireworks manufacturing was one of the major industries in Macau, with most of the firecrackers being exported. The rather eccentric office of Kwong Hing Tai Firecrackers was built over a pier jutting into the harbour.

9.4

The old Macau Labour Union Building, located on the praya of the Rua das Lorchas, is here shown with the national flag of the Republic of China flying from its roof in the 1950s.

9.5 & 9.6

These photographs of Pier 12 in Macau were taken in November 1964 and sometime in the 1950s respectively. This pier served ferry routes from Macau to Shantou. This area was often busy, with cargoes being loaded or unloaded, or congested with hundreds of passengers waiting for their slow boat to China.

9.7

The iconic symbol of Macau for four centuries, the old Mater Dei church built by the Jesuits as early as 1602. This church became the 'Ruins of St. Paul's' when the complex of buildings was destroyed by fire in 1835. The church's ruins and the adjacent archaeological remains of the old College of St. Paul are all that is left of the first western-style university in the Far East. Taken in September 1960, this photograph shows how few tourists visited this site in the post-war years; the people here seem to be mainly local women and children.

9.8

Another site of historical interest, the Kun-Yam Temple (Goddess of Mercy Temple) built in 1627, was the site of the first treaty signed between Ki Ying, the Viceroy of Canton, and Caleb Cushing, the United States Minister, on 3 July 1844. The rather dilapidated interior of the temple is shown here in 1960.

9.9

At the A-Ma Temple on 8 May sometime in the 1950s, when the temple was packed with people coming to worship Macao's most popular deity, the maiden A-Ma (also known as Tin Hau), the Goddess of Seafarers. The centuries-old A-Ma-Kao Temple gave the town its name in the sixteenth century when the Portuguese pronounced it Macao or Macau. Bus Route No. 5, with its ancient fleet of buses, ran all the way from the boundary post with China to the A-Ma Temple, an important transportation route for locals and visitors alike.

9.10

The A-Ma Temple was not always so busy.
At sunset in 1957, all is quiet in the area
and the temple looks quite desolate.

9.11

This 1950s photograph shows the corner of the Rua de Praia Grande and the lane leading up to the Travessa do Padre Narciso, with the garden of Government House behind its high walls. The towers of the Igreja de São Lourenço (St Laurence's Church) can be seen behind the Travessa do Padre Narciso.

9.12

The ancient fortress of Fortaleza do Monte before sunset in November 1964, with the Guia Lighthouse in the background. Situated near to the Ruins of St Paul's, the crumbling Fortaleza do Monte has always been a popular tourist destination. It was fully restored in the 1990s.

9.13

A view towards the centre of Macau from Penha hill in the 1950s, with the Jardim de Sao Francisco at the end of the tree-lined Praia Grande. Many Portuguese-style colonial buildings and churches can be seen along the hillsides.

The tree-lined Praia Grande curving around the Palacete de Santa Sancha at the end of the Macau peninsula in November 1964. This was an important military and political district under Portuguese rule, with the governor's official residence established in this grand old house since the late 1930s. Situated in verdant gardens on a semi-fortified terrace, the 'Governor's Palace' was typical of the homes built in previous centuries by the wealthy residents of Macau.

9.15

Walking along the Praia Grande to the Nan Van (Southern Bay) at the tip of the Macau Peninsula was a leisurely experience for many tourists in the 1950s.

9.16

A view from Igreja de São Lourenço in the 1950s, looking towards Wanzai with its piers along the inner Harbour. On the opposite shore was Mainland China.

9.17

A group of children help to make firecrackers by the roadside in 1963. They seem to be enjoying themselves, totally unaware of the perilous dangers of this industry.

9.18

Hawkers selling fruit and stationery on the
Rua do Tarrafeiro in September 1960.

9.19

The junction between Rua de Santo Antonio and Rua do Tarrafeiro in September 1960. A large and eye-catching Schweppes advertisement covers the entire side of this building. Schweppes soft drinks were produced in a new factory in Kwun Tong, Hong Kong, and exported to Macau for sale. The Chinese name of Schweppes was adopted from the last words of a beautiful Chinese poem: 'Every bottle as precious as gem, every drop as wonderful as elixir' (瓶瓶如珠玉，滴滴是甘泉).

9.20

Children on the verandah of a Portuguese-style house in September 1960 gaze out at the foreign photographer. Many of Macau's wonderful old buildings were in a state of advanced decay in the post-war period.

9.21

Walking through the narrow streets of Macau in September 1960, visitors might be attracted by the appetizing smell of beef entrails being cooked on hawkers' trolleys.

9.22

A scene captured on 5 February 1957 outside the Shing Cheong Lee oil and foodstuffs store. Neighbours are lingering outside the store to buy food and children are playing on the footpath. This image gives a sense of the dynamic and lively street life of old Macau.

9.23

Gambling was legalized in Macau in 1961, and by the 1970s the Lisboa Hotel and its casino had been built. The simple old culture of Macau gradually disappeared as new influences crept in from abroad. In the mid-1970s, a dance troupe from Paris began to perform in Macau, shocking some but delighting others. These entertainments were to become common attractions in Macau casinos in later years.

9.24

Scantily-clad French dance performances were first staged in Macau at the Teatro Dom Pedro V. From 1976 onwards, these performances transferred to the Mona Lisa Hall of the Lisboa Hotel. With alluring new attractions such as these, visiting Macau was no longer solely for outdoors sight-seeing. Much of the action in Macau had now moved indoors!

OLD HONG KONG
IN COLOUR

OTTO C.C. LAM